# Praise for *The C*

*a small sampling of testimonials given for the LIVE event that formed the basis of this book*

"It gave me goose bumps and brought tears to my eyes. I am so appreciative of this adventure! I am filled with so much love right now." —Rachael

"What a miracle. You've located all these wonderful people and brought them together. I hope you know how much your work is appreciated." —Linda

"What I needed to hear when I needed to hear it. Thank you. Thank you. Thank you." —Deborah

"The best awakening experience ever!! Such amazing tools! An experience beyond words!" —Leslie

"This is too much. The words are truly, amazingly healing... each syllable infused with love and truth, exactly like your core message. I feel I cannot even keep up. Thank you!!" —Mireille

"I was in tears the moment The Council began to speak! I feel so much lighter now! Thank you!" —Mary Ann

"Wow... just wow. So happy for this experience and growth that you have brought into my life!" —Debra Ann

"This is amazing! Daniel, I think your tones healed a hearing issue that has challenged me. Thank you! And thank you to The Council." —Pat

"I'm already planning on listening to this again right after it's over!" —Allison

"Thank you for always being so in tune with us and bringing us the wisdom and teachings to help us continue to expand and grow." —Kanaani

"This was amazing, direct, and profound. So, so, so good! Thank you for this experience." —Viktor

"Wow and wow! Loved it! With each episode we watch, I'm becoming so much more relaxed and excited, simultaneously!" —Rich

"This is wonderful! I gained so much from this experience. Thank you so very much, Mike, Lyssa, and Sasha. Great love and appreciation for you!" —Karri

"This was brilliant! As a teacher myself, I love how Bashar laid out the lesson, did a periodic review of his teachings, and gave clear, concise examples. 10 out of 10!" —Patrice

"This is the perfect summary of what is needed to experience a reality of joy, flow, and fulfillment. Love Bashar so much, love his clarity and conciseness." —Aaron

"Wonderful! I have learned so much from this communication and will now look at my life differently... with more hope and empowerment." —Lefi

"Excellent... clearly articulated, fundamental concepts for experiencing an amazing life. This all resonates with what I've come to understand from numerous sources and teachers, but I've never had it communicated so clearly and simply." —Karen

"Fantabulous stuff here, as expected." —Jamie

"I've listened to this three times and each time I get more and different feelings, impressions, and inspirations." —Marianne

"This was amazing. Blew my mind. Good thing my mind is an illusion." —Patty

"The Awakening Adventure is an incredible and rare first-hand opportunity to be in the presence of exceptional channelers and to hear the wisdom of those who speak through them. As a long-time follower of this type of information, I'd say it ranks as one of the best events I've had the privilege to attend." —Richard

"So grateful for this event! Feeling blissed-out, too, after this session with the beloved Arcturian Council. Thank you! Will be rewatching and relistening to these recordings and bathing in all their magnificent energies." —Abe

"O-o-o-h.... HOW EXCITING! The validation I received is thrilling. Now I'm in tears."—Carolyn

# The Great AWAKENING

# Also by Mike Dooley

**Books**

*An Adventurer's Guide to the Jungles of Time and Space* (formally titled *Lost in Space*)
*A Beginner's Guide to the Universe: Uncommon Ideas for Living an Unusually Happy Life*
*Channeled Messages from Deep Space: Wisdom for a Changing World* (with Tracy Farquhar; formerly titled *From Deep Space with Love*)
*Choose Them Wisely: Thoughts Become Things!*
*The Complete Notes from the Universe* (originally released in 3 volumes)
*The Dream, the Journey, Eternity, and God: Channeled Answers to Life's Deepest Questions* (with Sara Landon)
*Infinite Possibilities: The Art of Living Your Dreams*
*Leveraging the Universe: 7 Steps to Engaging Life's Magic*
*Life on Earth: Understanding Who We Are, How We Got Here, and What May Lie Ahead*
*Manifesting Change: It Couldn't Be Easier*
*Playing the Matrix: A Program for Living Deliberately and Creating Consciously*
*The Top 10 Things Dead People Want to Tell YOU*
*Totally Unique Thoughts: Reminders of Life's Everyday Magic*

**Card Decks**

*Notes from the Universe*
*Notes from the Universe on Abundance*
*Notes from the Universe on Love & Connection*

**Videos and Films**

*Manifesting Change*
*The Path Less Traveled*
*The Secret (featured contributor)*
*Thoughts Become Things*

**Online Adventures**

*The 21-Day Change-One-Thing Adventure*
*Playing the Matrix: A Laser Focused Series*
*A Trainer's Guide to Infinite Possibilities: Certification*
...and dozens more.

**For Children**

*Dreams Come True: All They Need Is You*
*Your Magical Life*

# The Great AWAKENING

## OUR PROPHESIZED TRANSFORMATION AND THE ATTAINMENT OF EMBODIED ENLIGHTENMENT

MIKE DOOLEY

**The Universe Talks**SM
Orlando, Florida, USA

Wholesale and foreign rights enquiries to: TGA@tut.com

1st edition, October 2024
10 9 8 7 6 5 4 3 2 1

Printed in the United States of America

Paperback ISBN: 978-0-9794739-0-6
E-book ISBN: 978-0-9794739-2-0
Audiobook ISBN: 978-0-9794739-1-3

Library of Congress Control Number: 2024909071

Cover design by Ralph Mojica
Interior design by Gina Tyquiengco

Photography credits:
Matt Kahn by Jessica Keener
Lyssa Royal Holt by Ronald Holt
Sara Landon by Lucia Kiel
Daniel Scranton by Lauren Stirpe

For Marisol

*"Whatever precious jewel there is in the heavenly worlds, there is nothing comparable to one who is Awakened."*

—Siddhartha Gautama, The Buddha

# Contents

A Word on Channeling ........ *xiii*
Foreword
It's the Perfect Illusion and Challenge ........ *xv*
Introduction ........ *xvii*
A Note on the Questions and Free Videos Link ........ *xxv*
Chapter 1
Thriving in New Landscapes of Consciousness
with Lyssa Royal Holt ........ 1
About Lyssa ........ 1
Thriving in New Landscapes of Consciousness ........ 2
Holographic Consciousness ........ 2
Density versus Dimension ........ 4
Understanding Your Ego ........ 9
Your Planetary Shift in Consciousness ........ 9
Doing the Work ........ 12
Meditations ........ 15
Chapter 2
Tapping into Your True Power
with Salvatore Rachele ........ 31
About Sal ........ 31
Tapping into Your True Power ........ 32
Reclaiming Your Power ........ 33
Remembering Your Power ........ 34
Standing in Your Power ........ 36
The Power of Rising Vibrations ........ 36
Working on Yourself ........ 38
Chapter 3
Living as an Ascended Master on Earth
with Sara Landon ........ 55
About Sara ........ 55
Living as an Ascended Master on Earth ........ 56
Your Force Field of Consciousness ........ 58
The Art of True Creation ........ 60
Levels of Consciousness ........ 63
Creating from Innocence ........ 70
Sleep, Pain, and Alzheimer's ........ 71

Chapter 4
The Role Love Plays in Self-Realization
with Matt Kahn ........................................ 75
About Matt ........................................ 75
Prelude ........................................ 76
Non-Trance Channeling ........................................ 76
The Ego, Higher Self, Spirit Guides, and Soul ........................................ 77
The Call to Awaken ........................................ 80
Set an Intention ........................................ 80
The Role Love Plays in Self-Realization ........................................ 80
The Divine Feminine ........................................ 80
The Divine Masculine ........................................ 82
Uniting Our Divine Energies ........................................ 82
Transmuting Trauma ........................................ 83
Embodied Love ........................................ 85
The Dimensions ........................................ 89
Dying in Order to Live ........................................ 91
More on the Ego and the Games It Plays ........................................ 92
Chapter 5
Developing the Gifts of Healing, Channeling, and Light Language
with Daniel Scranton ........................................ 99
About Daniel ........................................ 99
The Four Cornerstones of The 9D Arcturian Council Teachings ..... 99
The 9D Arcturian Council Message ........................................ 100
Developing the Gifts of Healing, Channeling, and Light Language 101
Being Awake ........................................ 101
How Did This All Get Started? ........................................ 102
The Journey and Meaning of Your Emotions ........................................ 103
Supernatural Gifts and Performing Miracles ........................................ 105
Tapping into Your Chakra System ........................................ 109
Ascension Symptoms ........................................ 110
Living Deliberately and Manifesting Consciously ........................................ 112
Chapter 6
The Self-Realization Tool Kit:
Everything You Need to Raise Your Vibration
with Darryl Anka ........................................ 125
About Darryl ........................................ 125
Darryl's Thoughts on Open (Extraterrestrial) Contact ........................................ 125

The Self-Realization Tool Kit:
Everything You Need to Raise Your Vibration ........ 127
The Five Universal Laws ........ 127
Your Destiny ........ 130
The Seven Basic Needs of Physical Life ........ 132
Life's Instruction Manual: The 5-Step Formula ........ 135
Finding Your Passion ........ 141
Synchronicity ........ 142
Abundance and Support for the Journey ........ 144
The Reflective Mirror ........ 144
Putting It All Together ........ 147
Epilogue
Enlightenment versus Transcendence ........ 157
Recommended Reading ........ 161
Acknowledgements ........ 164
About Mike Dooley ........ 165

# A Word on Channeling

Forty years ago, my mother told me she'd discovered some fascinating books by Jane Roberts. The author claimed to enter a trance state from which she would channel a disincarnate energy named Seth. During these sessions, her husband transcribed every word on the fly, ready for their publisher. I was genuinely concerned, telling her, *"I think you're losing it."* She snapped back, "Forget the source! Just read what Seth has to say, then judge!"

I did as I was told and so began the greatest journey of my life—inward.

In case you're as unfamiliar as I once was, channeling is the ability to intentionally alter your conscious focus to allow the spiritual energy of another from this density, dimension, *world*, plane, or others, to physically communicate through you—usually through writing or spoken word. There are many famous artistic and literary works whose creators claimed to have channeled them, including Michelangelo who said he could "see" the *Pieta* within the cold marble slab before taking up his chisel, Mozart who "heard" the music he would later compose, today's Abraham books written by Esther Hicks, *Jonathan Livingston Seagull* written by Richard Bach, and many others. Similarly, there are athletes who "get into a zone" to achieve peak performance. Interestingly, many holy books, including the Bible, are accepted by their followers to be the word of God or angels channeled by those whose names appear with each passage of scripture.

It's believed by some that we're all channels of our own inner essence, or spirit, through the physical instrument of our bodies. To think otherwise is to believe biological matter alone gives rise to our words, thoughts, personalities, and consciousness.

And did you catch my emphasis on "world" two paragraphs ago? Here I ask for your indulgence: in case it's not obvious, I do mean extraterrestrials (ETs). Isn't thinking we're alone in a Universe of one thousand trillion stars (not even counting planets) naïve? So… what to make of ETs? As Frank once shared with me, channeled by Tracy Farquhar, my coauthor of *Channeled Messages from Deep Space*: While we are unimaginably different than you, our spiritual and conscious evolution is nearly identical. There is *only* God, pure Source Energy, permeating the physical universe. Therefore, *all beings, from all worlds, are truly your spiritual brothers and sisters,* no matter their appearance or behavior.

In the chapters ahead, you will hear from several of these brothers and sisters.

Yeah... channeling has been around forever. It's prudent to caution, however, that just because information might be channeled doesn't necessarily mean it's true, relevant, or helpful. There are probably as many, if not more, lost souls beyond the veils of time and space looking for a mouthpiece as there are confused humans now walking the Earth. For myself, I discern whether something is worth embracing as truth with this little litmus test:

Does the information…

1) speak of life's beauty; or
2) speak of our power; and
3) is it non-exclusionary, leaving no one behind?

If you've read this far, I urge you to keep reading. Forget the source, if that helps—just read what the channels have to say. Then judge if the material is worthy of your consideration or even if it might transform your very life.

# Foreword

## It's the Perfect Illusion and Challenge

It's the perfect illusion and challenge: to be thrust into a space that you call reality with such a profound level of forgetting in favor of the possibility of creating, with free will, a new light to shine into eternity. A new version of everything: you. Because *you* are everything.

Welcome to the miracle of being human.

You are storytellers, but you've been telling yourselves the same stories over and over again. You don't read between the lines. You're literal—*literarily* literal.

You hear words and forget that they're vibrations floating through the space of nothingness. And you read, forgetting that you're simply seeing marks on paper, some of which absorb the light and some of which do not. You are not able, as we are, to hear or read past the words themselves and get the full transmission of the storyteller or author.

It is a limit, but one you can overcome. When you hear and see, listen and look for the energy between the words and the layers upon them. And be sure to also read with your heart as much as you do with your mind and your eyes so that you will truly understand.

You may ask, then: "What is there to do?"

There is nothing you must do.

Creation loves the fool and the wise man, and often they are one and the same. Creation loves the sinner and the saint for they, too, are the same. There can be no one and no thing that is not, in its full being, everything else at the same time. There is no right and wrong. There is only Is-ness. You cannot fail at being the one who is needed to complete the story of Infinity. Without you, exactly as you now are, the Universe would not exist.

So why this communication and the push toward waking those who sleep? Because too many are ready. *You are ready.* Ready to let go of suffering. Ready to become pure freedom. Ready to remember who you are. The game you have come here to play is to realize that *you are the Creator.*

Our choice to speak, like those within this book, is in part because of your request to receive these messages and to read them. *It's necessary in creation for all requests to be fulfilled.* It's also our pleasure to speak with you in this way for we see you as us, and to interact with another portion of ourselves is entirely satisfying. If some of the information that you have called through us helps accelerate your journey and place you in a position of feeling more well more of the time, then this, too, is our pleasure.

You will eventually come to find, however, that the information we share with you is nothing more than stopping someone who is frantically looking for their glasses and telling them, "They're already on your face."

We also hold a great level of curiosity for your mystery. We envy the possibility "to *not* know" as much as we do. From this not-knowing can stem true creation as you assemble all the components and weave the threads together in a way that is most pleasing to you. In our existence, this is no longer possible, as we see all the configurations simultaneously.

The arts, the way you weave words, and the stories you wrap around relationships and interactions are far more creative than we are capable of. To you, they are new. This is why so many come to be with you. Although we see each of you as us, and we see all your infinite possibilities, you yourselves choose in each moment which of those possibilities to apply. For us, these choices offer a moment of surprise in an existence [their own] that has made surprise unfamiliar. We thank you, as you are the best show on TV, so to speak, for we do not know the ending. We do not know what you'll do next.

—VAGREIN, channeled by JP (Jessie) Herman,
www.jpherman.com

# Introduction

I've always been intrigued by the stories of so-called "ascended masters" who've graced the face of the Earth: inspired by their miracles, wisdom, love, and the wild implication that what they've done, we can do—*and greater*. Jesus said as much.[1]

Whether naïve, hopeful, or both, I've always believed these tales to be true. And by this stage of my life, for reasons I'm about to share, I fully expect that one day soon others will attain a similar mastery over the elements—undoubtedly the wisest or most loving among us. I now even dare wonder, "Maybe even *me*…?" But where to begin? How to start?

Such musings were incomprehensible when I was a younger adult, especially since I knew of no creditable, modern stories of any such masters among us. Instead, I dove deep into my fascination with metaphysics[2] to live deliberately and create consciously (using creative visualization and learning of its supporting principles), and I've had a pretty stellar four decades at it. First, by practicing what I learned to thrive in my own life, and second, by writing seventeen books of my discoveries and hosting four world tours, teaching it to others. Though not without some setbacks and heartbreak. I was so fulfilled for so long that I began wondering with some concern, "Is this it? I mean, how many times does one travel to Tahiti in their life? And how

---

[1]King James Version of the Bible, John 14:12, "Verily, verily, I say unto you, He that believeth on me, the works that I do shall he do also; and greater works than these shall he do; because I go unto my Father."

[2]The *Oxford English Dictionary* defines metaphysics as the branch of philosophy that deals with the first principles of things, including abstract concepts such as being, knowing, substance, cause, identity, time, and space.

many millions of dollars are we to raise for our favorite charities?" The old answers of "more, better, faster" weren't hitting it for me anymore.

So, on December 16, 2018, sitting on a veranda overlooking the Bay of Manzanillo in Mexico, alone at home, I started making notes on my laptop. I began an online journal titled "Enlightenment," and in it, I entered about a half dozen of my favorite passages on the topic of "spiritual illumination" from a few of my favorite books, like *Illusions: The Adventures of a Reluctant Messiah* and *Jonathan Livingston Seagull*, both by Richard Bach; *Siddhartha* by Hermann Hesse; and *Ramtha: The White Book* by J. Z. Knight. This collection and my own related notes were to remind me that there could be much more to my life if I'd simply give these ideas more of my attention by returning to reread them from time to time.

Come January, however, I was back on the wheel of maya, entangled in the illusions, travel, and concerns of my life, until the following December. Back on that same veranda, I was slowly (and finally) making my way through *Autobiography of a Yogi* by Paramahansa Yogananda—overcome with bouts of euphoria as the weeks rolled by, stunned to be reading actual tales of yogis and their superhuman achievements chronicled by the author's life in this highly celebrated and much-respected international phenomenon.

And as if the rekindled excitement for my own hoped-for "self-realization" (another expression for enlightenment) wasn't already maxed out, I had a life-changing call with a woman named Sara Landon, serendipitously on December 16, 2019. She was a new acquaintance and channel of The Council, who told me during our scheduled session, without any earlier discussion of my interest in enlightenment, "You are undergoing an incredible shift into fully realizing yourself as the absolute master that you are. Every single one of you came here to be part of this great transformation of consciousness. You came to wake up: to come into the realization of the embodied masters that you are."

"*Me?*" I asked incredulously.

"Yes, YOU! You and many others because of where your collective consciousness now is. The next phase of your life will be a living mastery within the human experience before you officially take your seat at the table with the ascended masters." This was followed by sixty more minutes of further revelations, aha moments, and silent expressions of, "Oh my *God!*"

I hadn't been this excited since I was featured in *The Secret* by Rhonda Byrne.

The Council also spoke of where my inner work now lies: living more in the present moment, ending my addiction to logic, and learning to "open and allow" spirit to guide my actions (more on this in Sara's chapter). My ascension wasn't going to be effortless—at least not until I first laid the groundwork.

January swiftly arrived, along with the COVID-19 sequestrations, during which I found dozens more books on self-realization (see the Recommended Reading List in the back of this book), from which I constantly updated my own online journal. Of course, I still wrestled with my mortal dramas, as I do to this day, but I did so less and less. Journaling, reading, contemplating, and meditating became my new routines.

I've learned that spiritual enlightenment is indeed attainable, and yes, we—*you*—can and will *inevitably* experience it, in this lifetime or beyond. It's *not*, however, an endgame or an "all or nothing" achievement. Nor does ascension mean you suddenly move beyond the physical plane. It simply means you've raised your vibrations (more on this, too, in the chapters ahead). Still embodied and very much alive in the physical world, you continue to love and learn even more, ascending further, until you truly love all and self, or rather, *until you love all as self.* At which point, you'll either stick around to help others awaken—or you may choose to move beyond the physical plane.

I've long understood that we all wanted to be here, in these sacred, illusionary jungles of time and space, but now I better see that this was to enjoy them as they are and can be, not just to ascend our way out. The breathtaking and fleeting nature of our experiences here had not been known by God (All-That-Is or Divine Intelligence; not a God as portrayed by any religion I know of) until He thought to create and experience it *as us*. Being here on the razor's edge of reality creation is an extraordinary gift. Yet, as you can no doubt attest, when one is metaphorically "lost in space," the ride can be quite bruising, or worse. It can feel like life is happening *to you*, until you realize that you are happening *to life*, which is when you finally grasp that you and your thoughts are your life's only variable. Until then, a little bit of enlightenment (or a whole lot) would certainly add to the adventure.

Essentially, the wiser you become, the higher your vibrations, the easier life gets, and the greater your capacity to love. You'll experience ever-increasing levels of joy, clarity, energy, confidence, abundance, and miracle-making (overt, Jesus-like miracles—which will also be discussed in the chapters ahead). Eventually, your vibe will get so high and the love so intense, you'll literally glow (hence the stories of auras and halos), while other latent biological features are activated that will ramp up all your "clair" abilities (clairvoyance, clairsentience, etc.), halt physical aging, and unleash a plethora of other gifts and powers *now dormant within you, dear reader*. Are there not ancient teachings that say the same, offering that we are made in the likeness of God? Steeped in fear, however, we never came close to grasping the true meaning of this statement.

This natural evolution of consciousness will eventually lead to "burning bush moments" and quantum leaps forward—not just one, but many during our unending progression. Meanwhile, as Ram Dass said, "We're all just walking each other home," albeit still at a *very* early point in our spiritual learning curve, with home being a remembrance of and return to pure truth—the truth that we are all of the Divine, different lenses through which the same God sees, creators of our experience, bound by a love that far exceeds "love" as we've known it. We are not only one of many, but we are one *with* the source of many. Our false beliefs of separation will fall away, yielding a new unity consciousness. And, as with every mass migration, whether wildebeests on the Masai Mara or "sparks of God" playing small, there are forerunners. The latter are known as ascended masters.

Their example and teachings are to awaken us from the great sleep that befell spirit as it first conceived of and began exploring these jungles. They are the ones who choose to hang around after their illumination to help others, show us the way, and reveal who we really are and what we're truly capable of—as did The Buddha, for example, which literally translates to "The Awakened One."

"Inevitably" sure sounds good—but who wants to wait?! At the very least, we can now begin moving toward our own awakening with awareness, desire, and will, which is what this book is about. Surprisingly (at least for myself), as The Council and all the channels fluent on this topic teach, you cannot find realization through the brain or the mind. In the words of Sasha, channeled by Lyssa Royal Holt in chapter 1, "Enlightenment is not something you do; it's more of an *undoing*." It's an allowing achieved through a profound, waking relaxation and recognition of life's absolute, utter perfection.

Of course, there's even more to the equation than meets the eye. As gods ourselves, far more than we presently know ourselves to be, there are other realms, dimensions, and parallel universes of which we're also a part but no longer aware. Some we came from; others are beyond our comprehension. All filled with their own self-reflecting sparks of God—*adventurers*, much like us—some physical, others ethereal. Most of whom are further along than us *spiritually* and technologically. Many are even aware of us and our continued slumber of confusion; they were once where we are now in terms of our spiritual evolution and awakening—true family members on the path.

Motivated by love, they eagerly wish for us to know more of our origins, the possibilities that exist for our fullest expression, and to accelerate our own embodied enlightenment. So they whisper to us through automatic writing, channeling, in the sleep state, or any other way they can—sometimes leaving clues or signs, other times infusing us with ideas and inspiration when we least expect it. Careful not to give too much too soon, or the romance of our adventure might be spoiled, like turning on a light in a darkened movie theater. They also don't want to risk our overreliance on them, preferring to cultivate our own ingenuity and resourcefulness. Ours are the kind of lessons we must learn for ourselves, although asking for and receiving their help, they say, is allowed. This is the tightrope they walk—responding to the anguished cries of humanity over millennia, yearning to encourage and empower us, while not crossing a line that would do the exact opposite.

They bring forth some of the most relevant and exciting clarity now available concerning our potential and the very nature of reality. And, not coincidentally, relating it to the rising energies now sweeping planet Earth: changes that were prophesized long ago by seers like Nostradamus, The Book of Revelation, and the ending of the ancient Mayan calendar (which signified the less celebrated, if even acknowledged, beginning of a new one).

This is the Age of Aquarius, "a time when humanity takes control of the Earth and its own destiny as its rightful heritage, with the destiny of humanity being the revelation of truth and the expansion of consciousness… some people will experience enlightenment in advance of others and therefore be recognized as the new leaders in the world."[3]

The puzzle pieces are finally coming together.

Herein, you will learn from six such voices of truth, living channels who speak the language of "awakening through mastery of self." World-renowned mystics who, along with those they speak for, wish to help us help ourselves. Not to dispel the illusions of time and space, but to help you sooner have conscious dominion over them, as pioneers of the human race. Our sessions were part of a 2022 live, online event that included more than three thousand attendees. Every week for six weeks I featured a single guest, each channeling higher vibrational beings—some presently living a physical existence, albeit from other star systems, and others non-physical.

My own assimilation of life's truths has been profoundly accelerated by learning from *different* teachers—even when, as you're sure to find, there may appear to be contradictions between them. Yet, with a little time to dwell upon their perspectives, invariably there will follow a burst of clarity from which their differences merge into a more complete understanding of what it means to awaken. You'll also find that some of their teachings may only seem to be indirectly related to awakening, focusing on ideas and techniques that can help us better navigate time and space, to more deliberately live our lives, as we learn to harness our power—which actually makes their teachings directly related to awakening.

These are exciting yet pivotal times. All of us are facing new forks in the road of our lives. Resistance to change and new ideas can be seen boiling over in the streets and among nations, bringing to our attention long-overlooked imbalances, *which means they can finally be healed.* Even COVID-19 marked the beginning of a great healing, forcing most of humanity to rearrange their priorities. Everything, even the painful and ugly, has a gift for us, exactly the one we'll most benefit from; such is the poetic nature of the Universe.

The questions before us are simple: To continue living as "merely human" or to live supernaturally? To see yourself as separate from everyone or to recognize our unity? To be motivated by fear or inspired by love? We can literally see the camps set up around the world where others have made their choices. The apocalypse is at hand—the

[3]Vera W. Reid, *Towards Aquarius*

final confrontation between the light of truth and our prehistoric ignorance. "Final," because ignorance is on its last legs. Every day in the news we see the biblical metaphor of people being ideologically separated like wheat from the chaff through their own choices. Those prepared to do the inner work necessary for illumination (and our numbers are rising exponentially), will gain mastery over the physical world—thy kingdom shall come, thy will shall be done, on Earth as it is in "heaven."

May the words that follow help you realize who you really are, what you're truly capable of, and how to live at all times guided by love within the sacred eternal now. May they help you remember that you are, and have always been, the eyes and ears of the Divine come alive in the dream of life. An awakening process otherwise known as enlightenment, self-realization, illumination, ascension, soul integration, and Christ Consciousness—the fabled, misunderstood, and long-awaited Second Coming.

Yours in the adventure,

## A Note from the Universe[sm]

*One of the most comforting thoughts of all is knowing that all roads lead home.*

*Even more comforting is finally understanding that you never left.*

*From all of us "back home,"*
The Universe

# A Note on the Questions Asked in Each Chapter

Each chapter contains questions and answers that were exchanged during the live sessions mentioned in the introduction. Some of these questions were asked by me and some by audience members.

To make it clear who asked the question, audience member questions will start with a speech bubble icon (💬) and be enclosed by quotation marks. Questions without this were asked by me.

# Free Videos

Each of the featured channels in this book partook in a live online event that created the content of this book. Free clips of their in-trance broadcasts are available for our readers: www.tutadv.club/tgav

# Chapter 1

## Thriving in New Landscapes of Consciousness *with Lyssa Royal Holt*

### About Lyssa

Lyssa has been a seminar leader, channel, and author since 1985. She is the co-director, with husband, Ronald Holt, of Seed of Life Institute LLC and the SOLi School, an organization whose primary purpose is assisting individuals understand the nature of consciousness and to put this understanding into practice in daily life—providing a road map to the process of realizing true awareness beyond the human identity.

Lyssa is best known for her in-depth explorations on the nature of extraterrestrial consciousness and how it impacts human evolution. Her books *The Golden Lake*, *The Prism of Lyra*, *Visitors from Within*, *Preparing for Contact*, and *Millennium* are classics in the field of channeled literature, as well as her highly acclaimed *Galactic Heritage Cards*—a one-of-a-kind set of 108 inspirational cards based on the cosmology she introduces in her classic book *The Prism of Lyra*. She also has an extensive library of audio material based on her work since the late 1980s. She has been interviewed on TV and radio around the globe (including by the Discovery Channel, Shirley MacLaine's radio show, and *Interview with E.D. ExtraDimensionals* on Gaia TV). She has appeared in countless magazine articles over the last three decades (and counting).

Lyssa channels Sasha, a fourth density Pleiadian female. Sasha extends an aspect of her consciousness to Lyssa for communication during appropriate times, with students and clients, even as she (Sasha) tends to her own life elsewhere in this physical universe.

In the following text, Sasha will refer to herself as "we" as she shares her knowledge about how you can thrive in new landscapes of consciousness. She breaks this down into four parts: holographic consciousness, planetary shift in consciousness, doing the work, and meditations.

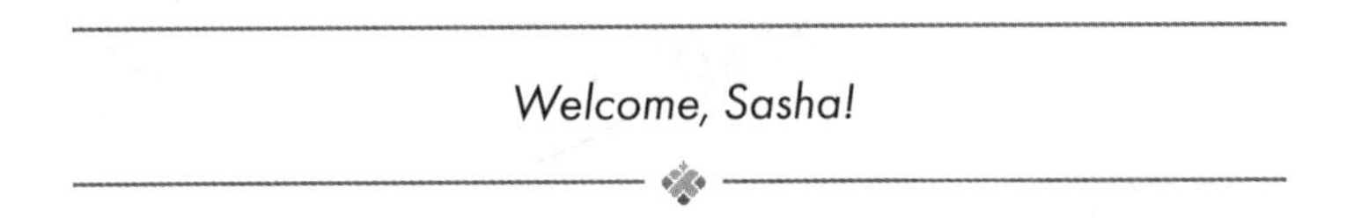


Greetings, my friends. It's an honor to be invited to share with you.

## Thriving in New Landscapes of Consciousness

### Holographic Consciousness

We're first going to give you some metaphors to help you understand the nature of consciousness so that you can better understand what's happening on Earth at this time of accelerated evolution. We like to use metaphors because language is a very constrained tool that does not really express the nature of the truth that is beyond the time-space reality.

First, let's look at the idea that you have probably heard called *Oneness*. What does that really mean? It's a nice, airy-fairy concept, but what is it based on?

We want to introduce you to the idea of holographic consciousness. Imagine that you have a regular photograph of an apple in your hands. Then, imagine that you tear up that photo, and you spread the pieces all over a table. In order to reassemble the image of the apple in your reality, on the physical plane, you'd need to gather each of those pieces of the photograph, much like a puzzle, and paste them together. This is how you see reality in your limited time-space state.

Now, imagine you have another photograph of an apple, and you tear it up into many pieces. However, this time, we're beginning with a holographic photograph, which means that when you pick up each of those separate pieces that you've torn up and you look at them, the complete image of the apple is still there. And if you were to tear up those pieces some more, you'd find that no matter how small you tear them up, each would still have the complete image of the apple. This means that every piece is a fractal of the original holographic pattern.

Consciousness is exactly the same. So when we say there is really only one consciousness in creation that is meant literally using the metaphor we've just talked about. You are like the image of the complete apple. You, as individual beings, are like little fractals of the One, like the little pieces that appear to be torn away. Somehow, you have convinced yourselves that you are separate, that Oneness is something out there to someday, maybe, achieve.

In your evolution and awakening process, many of you are beginning to suspect that you are a hologram of the One consciousness. This will make it possible for you to also understand yourself as part of this Oneness, from which you can begin living with a dual consciousness. This means that while you are aware of yourself having chosen a physical lifetime, at the same time you can also possess the awareness of yourself as the complete apple, or the complete hologram.

This is a necessary and important bridge. This dual awareness will enable you to eventually operate more and more from the realm of the whole, or the One, rather than from the individualized self.

This awakening is a process. The first step, you could say, is the intellectual understanding. More significantly, however, is achieving an emotional understanding through your experience. This may happen perhaps through meditation or even through what we call contact work, which is you contacting us or the angelic realms, for example, in sessions like this one. When you do, your intellectual knowledge can then become visceral wisdom within your being, and that is when consciousness changes.

Practice and play with this idea of yourself as the hologram, even though you've fooled yourself into believing you're a singular being.

---

*The dual consciousness: Is that ego and Higher Self?*

---

You could label them that way, yes, but it is way more than that. Actually, you are jumping a little bit ahead of where we're going. You're correct in the sense that as long as you are in a physical body, you are going to have some type of mechanism that creates individuality. At the same time, what you call Higher Self never goes away, nor is it something "out there." It's another version of you. It isn't really a "self" at all—it is a field of awareness. As you refine your awareness, you'll begin living more from the Higher Self field, or the hologram, and less from the ego, or the individualized self.

## Density versus Dimension

Now, let's sort out the whole idea of dimension and density. As you know, different teachers and channels use different words [including in this very book], sometimes for the same things, creating a little bit of confusion. However, as you sit with what we have to share with you on these ideas, you'll begin to feel the One truth being expressed through all the channels in various creative ways, no matter what words are chosen.

If consciousness is really One, imagine it, then, emanating the brilliance of a pure, white light. Imagine also a crystal or a prism that you put near that white light, which would serve as the separation mechanism. As the white light passes through the prism, voilà: you have a rainbow.

Any rainbow you see in your physical reality after a rainstorm is a perfect example of this. If you look closely at one, you'll notice seven light frequencies in the colors. If you look really closely, you'll see that those frequencies are not sharply divided, but they actually blend and flow into each other to create the full spectrum.

We can apply this idea to the One consciousness as it went through its process of fragmentation. As consciousness went through a similar separation process to create the physical universe, seven *densities* were created—we'll share more on this terminology later. Each of the densities represents a different characteristic of consciousness, from the most separated (unaware) to the most integrated (fully aware). This also includes the type of consciousness, for example, that makes up the very building blocks of your reality, such as atoms, molecules, and the like. Most of this information goes beyond the scope of this chapter, but for those curious, we share more about it in our book *The Prism of Lyra*.

When you're experiencing this separation as a physical being, it feels as if you are focused in one life in one reality, and all other lives are in a different time. However, your consciousness is actually expressing itself in all the other "rainbow colors" of density simultaneously. Two of these densities—the third and fourth—have particular importance for what we are about to talk about next.

On your world, planet Earth, for the last many thousands of years, you've been experiencing the greatest level of separation possible, which is third density. It's why you forget who you are and your connection to the Universe. You live in a very polarized reality, often fighting each other, and you feel very, very alone and disconnected. You are now experiencing the transition to a new state of consciousness: fourth density. This is when your deep sense of separation, aloneness, and polarity begins shifting into a more integrated reality. Most *physical* civilizations go through this evolutionary process.

This evolutionary process takes a while, but your civilization has very recently gone into one of the most intense transitional phases of the process, which probably will not surprise many of you.

This is what we mean by how the concept of density describes the characteristics of consciousness. The characteristics of third density display more separation and polarity. The characteristics of fourth density include the beginnings of integration, healing, and expanded awareness of the One. Ego is stronger in third density and weaker in fourth density. In the following graphic, you can see a representation comparing the densities.

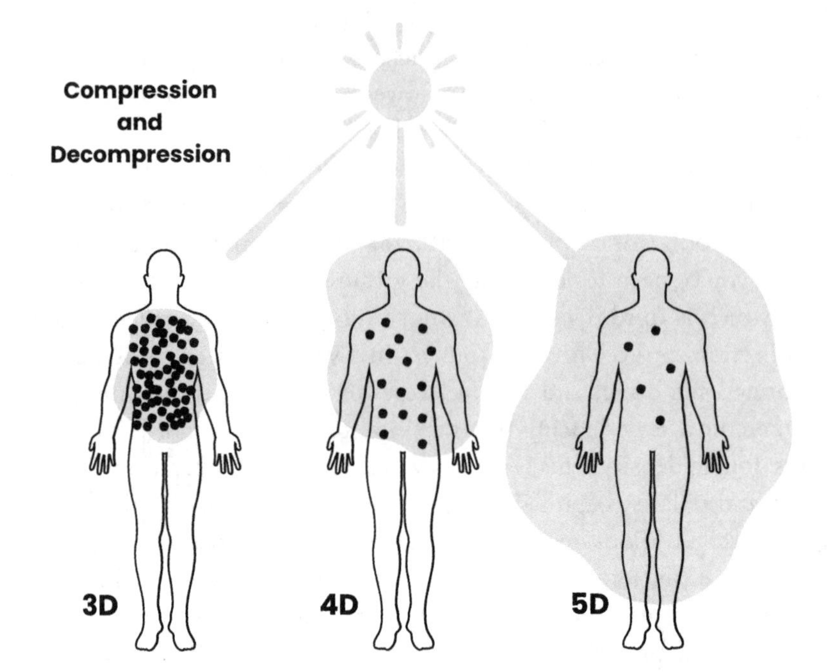


The density of the black dots represents how tightly compacted matter is in that density. This is not something that's measurable with any of your modern instruments. It may better be understood as an energetic density. On the left, for third density, you can see that the light of your being (often referred to in spiritual circles as prana or chi) doesn't have a lot of room to move around. It is limited in its expansion due to the denseness of matter. This is the reason for the term *density*. Matter is very, very densely focused energy.

In the middle, when you move into fourth density, you can see that matter begins to decompress, or open, and the prana now has more room to grow and expand, which mirrors the expansion of consciousness in this density. This prana is your own light as a part of the light of the Universe. It is not anything outside of you. As you move into higher densities, this expansion continues. For example, in fifth density there's even more light with an even greater decompression of matter and, thus, an even more dramatic expansion of consciousness. At some point, physical incarnation no longer occurs, and consciousness is no longer anchored by the denseness of matter.

So where does dimension come into this?

If density represents the *quality or characteristics* of consciousness, then we see dimension as the *container or envelope* in which that consciousness has its experience. Your third dimension, like third density, has a lot of limitations and structure built into it. This ensures that you eventually have the experience of going within to awaken yourself instead of being distracted by the outer world, which reinforces separation like a looping cycle. Ultimately, the number of dimensions is infinite because there are infinite types of containers in which you can experience consciousness. You will experience the container that is most necessary for your greater evolution. Please do not be concerned about what dimension you are in, as it is ultimately unimportant. This is something directly related to states of consciousness and what is needed to reach your evolutionary potential.

---

*I'd love to better understand "dimension." The envelope in our case would be planet Earth. I believe Earth is in the third dimension right now, but individually, we're each experiencing slight differentiations of our own density, which is rising. Therefore, somebody could be fourth density while living in a third dimensional world.*

*The envelope is the stage we're all sharing right now, which is also increasing in vibration. So, in a way, the adventure before us is to raise our own density to match, or even lead a little bit, the vibration of the Earth so that we can individually possess a density that's going from third to fourth or maybe even fifth. I've come to understand that one can't be too far from the dimension that's containing you.*

*Perhaps you could confirm two things: one, when you say "envelope," you mean the stage we're all sharing—planet Earth in our case; and two, our planet has a single dimensional vibration, whereas each of us has a unique individual density vibration.*

Yes, we would agree with what you've said, and we're going to give you one more thing to think about. If the envelope becomes too "small" for the growing consciousness, then, in a sense, you burst forth from that envelope into a new "larger" envelope, which is indeed the experience of shifting dimensions. However, we must remind you that trying to understand this from the perspective of a human mind bound to time will give you a headache!

You on Earth are sharing a common experience of transitioning from third to fourth density. The collective consciousness of the planet (a species identity made up of frequency, if you will) can only express a frequency in which all beings are able to resonate—like a median frequency. On an individual level, however, there are individuals expressing far below and far above the median. This is a simplified explanation, but it's meant to demonstrate how you are very connected to each other, yet you also have your own trajectories of evolution as individuals.

---

*I don't want to make this complicated. But if we find ourselves expressing in a higher dimensional vibration while still on Earth, would we leave the lower vibrational dimension physically? Would we physically disappear, as I've heard from other teachers?*

No, no, no. The idea of disappearing and shifting in that way is the mind's attempt at trying to understand this process. Consider, for example, the Mike that existed thirty or forty years ago. Is he the same in consciousness as the Mike that exists today? Did the earlier Mike disappear from reality somewhere? There really is only One consciousness that is emanating a unique experience in every conceivable variable of reality simultaneously. In that way, there are infinite Mikes and Lyssas. Nevertheless, there is really only One—this One isn't any of those individual identities, yet it contains them all.

We are speaking of an evolutionary process of perception and expansion of awareness. Remember, what you see around you will always be a reflection of yourself and the life you're creating in this emanation of you. You're not going to see things pop in and out of reality (because there isn't really an *objective* reality to move in and out of). You will instead see a change happening in your reality, your experience, as *you* grow.

Most importantly, you will feel a change within you. Most of the time you won't really be able to put your finger on what that change is. It just feels different—which we know many of you are experiencing now. The innate wisdom of the One that is always in balance organizes this process so, in a sense, there is really nothing for you to do except relax, remember your true nature, and enjoy the ride.

## Understanding Your Ego

If you are naturally One consciousness, One light, how is it possible to condense yourself into an individualized being and have an experience as a singular identity? In some ways, you are like a fictional character in the landscape of the hologram. How do you create such an illusion that shapes your experience?

This is where the ego comes in. The ego is neither negative nor positive but simply a mechanism. It is a mechanism, like an anchor that keeps you rooted and grounded into a separated reality. It therefore stands to reason that in a third density reality, where it's so very dense and separated that you've even forgotten who you are, you would need a very heavy anchor to be able to have that separative experience. The good news is that as you move into a fourth density reality, that anchor becomes lighter and lighter.

This is what you're now experiencing through your evolution. The ego is quite comfortable being anchored, and so, as the galactic and universal energies are compelling you to move toward integration and evolution, it feels resistance in letting go. It is one of the reasons why you have such power struggles on Earth. This is just a small challenge along the way that you have already begun working through.

## Your Planetary Shift in Consciousness

There's a huge shift in consciousness now happening on Earth. What is causing it? This transformation can be understood by comparing it to the seasons of a year.

Your planet experiences different qualities of existence during each of the seasons. In the winter season, for example, a lot of things go to sleep or go dormant, and in the spring and summer, lots of things start to bloom.

Your planet (and others) experiences great galactic evolutionary cycles of consciousness that are very much like seasons. Your great galactic cycle is approximately twenty-six thousand years long. During the past thirteen thousand years, you've been in what is like a deep autumn and winter cycle. In this type of cycle, you have the sense of being in a much more separated and dormant state of consciousness growth. This is where the concept of "the fall" came from—that humanity "fell" into a state of sleep in which you appear to have forgotten your divine nature. In 2011–2012, you hit the crossover point where you've exited that phase, and you have begun to move into a spring cycle of consciousness on your world. This was, and still is, the dawning of fourth density consciousness on Earth.

This means that you are now shaking off the amnesia and thawing yourself out from the winter, while seeds that were planted thirteen, fourteen, and even fifteen thousand years ago are now starting to blossom. This blossoming will continue for the next thirteen thousand years. During this time, you will be healing all the old baggage that's no longer necessary, and if you gain enough momentum through your healing and awakening process in this early part of the cycle, you will create enough energy for a full jump into a fourth density consciousness as a planetary species. Right now, many of you are making that transition as much as you can in your small envelope—while Earth is presently shaking off third density and moving into fourth.

When you metaphorically move from winter into spring, from being totally asleep with deep amnesia to awakening, there are core lessons and concepts to pay attention to. Honing your understanding in these areas will give you traction for accelerated learning and far greater peace of mind as you move into fourth density, because the old ways of doing things in third density will simply not work anymore.

### *Mind and Consciousness*

The most important thing to help facilitate this change is learning the difference between mind and consciousness. In third density reality, when you're the most separated, you almost exclusively operate through the mind. However, at such a dense frequency, the mind is more effective at surviving than in remembering the true nature of reality. Mind and ego are well-suited to helping you navigate your deep sense of separation, leading you in your initial steps through that tunnel of compression in third density. Mind and ego are not able to be your guides into the new fourth density reality, no matter how much they try.

This is all starting to shift now. There are new energies available to you. What you're being called to do is to go through a process of intuitive self-observation. One of the most important things to learn is the difference between mind and consciousness. Thoughts, beliefs systems, and judgments are all of the mind. Imagine them like clouds in the sky, with the sky being your open, expanded, limitless consciousness. The clouds, the airplanes, the birds, and the pollution *in* the sky are like the mind *within* your consciousness. We'll talk a little bit more about how to work with this later.

### Navigating with Your Heart

In third density, you've become very accomplished at navigating your life with the mind and the ego, which is also very much solar plexus energy. You've learned to push your way through with the will of the ego to get things done. However, we've spoken to so many of you who are noticing now that this doesn't work anymore. You are beginning to see that when you push yourself the way you used to do even a few short years ago, it actually hurts and is no longer effective.

The transition that is now happening means that you'll find far greater success moving less from a solar plexus, or egoic, way of navigation into more of a heart-centered, or energy-centered, way of navigation. This is very, very different. This has more to do with going with the flow: the flow of life, of energy.

We think you know this difference and how it feels in your body. You know what the compression feels like when you're trying to operate from a mental doing-doing-doing place. Conversely, you also know the freedom and relaxation you feel when you're in the flow: things just come together, and you move in a very smooth way.

### Will versus Flow

And finally—this is connected to navigation—let's look at will versus flow.

Now is the time to familiarize yourself and begin practicing being more sensitive to where the flow is and to put your energy there. When you try to use your will but find the flow isn't there, you may even feel constriction or pain. When you feel that energetic resistance, back away, try something else, and find the flow. Remember, stasis or quiet is also an option, and, at times, it's necessary as well.

## Doing the Work

What is the work? For this period now, as you're starting to move into fourth density reality, most of you already feel a need to shift or adjust your life because you are feeling the difference in energy. However, you may be at a loss regarding where to begin. What follows are some ideas and meditations to get you started. Some people bristle at hearing the word "work." It never has to be a burden, but it is necessary to help you develop a sense of self-responsibility for your own growth. Also, in this phase of your evolution, the ego still has a need to feel useful. When it believes it's doing "work," it cooperates more! This, too, will pass, and you will find that "work" and "play" simply merge into your *being* in the now.

### *Finding the Flow*

As we just reviewed, it's important you begin to grasp the difference between mind and consciousness. Going forward, we encourage you, day by day, even hour by hour, especially when you feel the urge to begin a project at home or work, to check in with yourself and notice whenever you feel stuck. In those moments, give yourself some time to really look within and see where you're trying to push or force something with the mind or the will, and see if you can instead relax into your being to feel the flow and move that way instead.

### *Seeing the World as a Mirror*

Another idea that becomes *very* important as you move into fourth density is the recognition that you are living in a reflective Universe. This means that the "bad guy" out there that triggers you is not some rogue part of God or the Universe. It is simply an unloved, unrecognized, unintegrated aspect of *yourself.*

We don't mean for you to become neurotic or obsessed with having to intellectually figure out what every reflection in your life means and what you're supposed to do about it. It's more of an intuitive process for when you encounter something that triggers you.

When you do encounter something that sets you off, try to begin working with it as a mirror. This mirror shows you something that, like a gift, is being given (from yourself to yourself) to benefit your own integration process, if you let yourself receive it.

In the world today, with all the craziness happening externally, it's very easy to get caught up in these dramas and want to take sides. But that's just going to keep you in a polarized reality and focusing on the outer world when it is necessary to begin training your focus inward. We're not talking about ignoring the external world. We're talking about not getting emotionally swept away and triggered by it. Instead, use such catalysts to see yourself more clearly and to heal more deeply. You will do so by integrating those parts of yourself that were separated.

### *Performing Miracles*

We know there is a lot of talk in some spiritually-minded circles about special powers, let's say, bilocation and—

*Ascension! Shapeshifting! Teleportation! Telekinesis! Telepathy!*

We know this really floats your boat and we have a big smile for you for that, but you know what we've told you previously: *inner mastery always comes before mastery of the external world.*

Returning to the idea of the reflective universe, we can say that as you learn to focus inward and master yourself, then you'll start to see what would have previously been called miracles. When you're focusing outward and trying to manipulate reality, *it blocks the whole process.* Your priority then, obviously, is to begin healing yourself. When the miracles start showing up, recognize they're simply a by-product of the inner work you've done.

### *Healing the Emotional Body*

Healing the emotional body is a hugely significant piece of the awakening puzzle. The very simple analogy we're going to give you is that if you have a huge suitcase filled with stuff, your so-called baggage, and you're trying to go through a very tiny door, you will have to drop the suitcase in order to get through the door.

When we say drop the suitcase, we're not talking about ignore, deny, reject, judge, or hate what's in the suitcase. We're talking about the necessity of unpacking what's in it once and for all and sorting through all those things for which there may still be emotional attachments, be they positive or negative. It's time to create a new relationship with them. This new relationship is one of appreciation, gratitude, and love for those heavy things that have given you some very good spiritual muscles.

In the last thirteen thousand years, you have experienced a lot of trauma. We are just talking about on Earth; we're not even including the multitude of lifetimes you've had on other planets. There have been a lot of painful experiences and emotions that are now being unlocked for the healing process to begin. It can seem like a daunting, impossible task. But this is not a linear process. You don't have to unpack each and every thing and look at it individually. That *would* take millennia upon millennia. The kind of healing we're encouraging happens more on a holographic level. The first place where any kind of healing happens is in the here and now, with your physical body.

We'd like you to begin considering your physical body as a tool for emotional healing. You can use your somatic senses—meaning the senses that help you feel what's going on in your body—as a way to really accelerate this healing process. Illustratively, if you have a chronic physical condition, it's very often related to what's been held emotionally in the body either in this life or over many lifetimes. Many of you already know this, yet it's often frustrating because many people who feel like they don't know how to access their emotional trauma forget to use their physical body as a guide. This is why we say your body, in the here and now, is your time capsule where you can access everything.

Whatever is showing up in your body is like the combination lock that can help you access the withheld energy from past trauma or pain and begin to release it. We are going to give you a very simple meditation exercise shortly that you can use to practice this process.

### *Ascension or Integration*

This brings us to the question, "What is ascension or awakening?" It has also been called enlightenment, soul integration, or self-realization.

We usually don't like to use the term *ascension* simply because of the connotations. Many people think it means not facing what needs to be faced and disappearing into the ether or flying off on a spaceship. It has more to do with raising one's vibrations through consciousness evolution. This vibrational change happens as you heal, all while remaining you, embodied, and fully embracing where you are in the here and now. This is what this work is all about.

We prefer, as you've already noticed, to use the word *integration.* Integration means that you come into your wholeness, rather than leaving behind a part of you that you dislike. It's the bringing together and the embracing of all your parts and experiences that have previously been denied. This is dealing with that big suitcase as you face the little door through the unpacking, sorting, and embracing process. In that embrace, the healing unfolds.

For us, ascension *is* integration. Let us look, for example, at the difference between humans on Earth right now and myself, Sasha. I'm fourth density and still have a body, so what is the difference in our experience of reality compared to yours?

In my civilization, partly because we are older, we have had the time and made the effort to unpack and heal for this integration. Because of this, we can recognize ourselves as more integrated beings in an experiential way. That's the main difference. This is where you are now moving. Yet, between here and there, you must do the work. The fact that you are hearing or reading these words means that you've already begun.

### Meditations

All this talk is fine, but if you don't apply it in your life, if you don't use it in some way, what good is it really?

We would like to share some tools to assist you. The first meditation will help you experientially learn the difference between mind and consciousness. Your intellectual mind probably understood what we said about this, but we have found that humans need to repeatedly feel an experience to really understand something on a deep level.

### *Sky Meditation*

After relaxation, begin the meditation by imagining that you are in an airplane during takeoff.

Feel the plane flying upward at an angle, and then it begins to pass through some clouds. You feel a little bumpiness or turbulence, representing the thoughts in your mind. Then, you reach a level altitude flying high above the clouds.

This imagery represents mind and consciousness. The sky represents your consciousness and is unlimited in all directions. The illusion, however, is that it's a dome or has a perimeter—even though it doesn't. Your thoughts and distractions (mind) are like clouds in that sky. They are temporary and change shape, so it isn't necessary to see them as your true identity.

As much as you can, allow yourself to simply abide in this space of the sky. It represents pure, live awareness without separation. The sky represents the One we spoke of earlier—your holographic consciousness. You, as a separated being, are a fractal of the One.

As you rest here and meditate, thoughts are going to arise from the mind. This is normal. It's natural. Maybe some emotions will arise. Each time anything like that shows up and distracts you, remind yourself it's like a cloud passing through the space of the sky—your true awareness or your true self.

As you practice this more and more, it'll begin to affect your daily life because when your mind starts getting cluttered or busy, you'll intuitively remember that you are the sky. This can help bring you back to that space: the place of spacious awareness that you really are.

Some might think this meditation is simplistic or even boring. This is because the ego and the mind are constantly busy and trying to distract you from silence. This can be an extremely powerful meditation for retraining yourself to tune in more to the vibration of your consciousness instead of being dragged around by the thoughts of the mind. With repeated practice, you'll find greater and greater peace as you experience your consciousness like the sky, and when the mind gets busy, you will viscerally feel how disharmonious it is to your well-being. You'll begin to crave the peace and expansiveness of the sky.

### *Breathing Meditation*

This meditation will help you to use the somatic experiences of your body to release stored energy, emotions, and trauma.

We're going to give you a basic outline for this meditation. As you use it, you must be really willing to adapt it to your circumstance because it's a fluid experience rather than a fixed one. For example, let's say you have chronic knee pain in your right leg. As you sit in your meditation, bring your attention to the pain, almost as if you have a nose on your knee. You will breathe in and out through that knee. That's all you need to do. Your Higher Self will then take the reins for this healing.

As you do this, old emotions or thoughts might come up. Just let them be like clouds passing by. What you're doing is releasing stored energy, like releasing gas when you open a bottle of soda. When you use your consciousness and connect it with your breath on the physical body, you start opening areas in your energy body to allow stored and trapped energy to be set free. Sometimes you may notice the release, especially if emotions arise or if you're sensitive to energy. Other times, you may not feel anything. The effects are cumulative, so be consistent in your practice.

If you don't have a physical ailment but it's more of an emotional condition that you'd like to release, such as anxiety that presents as a tightness in the chest, then just bring your attention to the general area of the chest or the tightness. Simply use your intuition when choosing where to bring your attention and do the breathing there. The location may change from time to time.

Both the sky and breathing meditations will take you on a journey that is different for everyone. They each offer a powerful place to get started on the integrative journey back to wholeness.

---

*Changing the subject, where are you right now, physically speaking? In the Pleiades? On a ship of some sort?*

Right now, my team has been within the Earth's orbit for many, many years because of the work we're doing, which includes preparing the Earth for [ET] contact. We're a little bit off in frequency compatibility, so we are not visible at this time (though we can change that, if needed). We are usually over the area of Japan.

---

*Unbelievable and crazy cool! It hints at the scope of reality and what's possible.*

*I heard you earlier, loud and clear, about inner mastery coming before mastery of the physical universe. I'm ready to do the work, whatever it takes. And I'd imagine our live and future audience members do, or will, feel the same. Yet, for me, I don't know where my pain is. I love my life and things are humming along really well. I don't know where I've deluded or kidded myself, what I've suppressed or hidden. I don't know where I've stored that heavy suitcase, yet here I am yearning for an awakening that is my birthright and not finding it. Clearly, I'm missing something. I'd love some ideas to gain traction.*

You don't have to go searching with your shovel and dig really deep in an endless search to find your suitcase. What's more important is to let yourself be available when any issues or pain show up. When that happens, simply work with them. The most important thing is just being willing and available, so that when the opportunity comes, you can jump on it, as you say.

One little hint is that adults can often find their pain by remembering it as a child. Over time, the ego creates defense mechanisms, elaborate stories, and belief systems to protect those early wounds, so they become unrecognizable as an adult. Everyone has blind spots when they try to view themselves. This is why we gave you the meditation of working with the somatic experience of the body as a way to unlock the old pain or see what you need to see. Your body stores this pain, and as you get older, if it is ready to be released, it starts giving you little hints through bodily manifestations.

*I loved reading The Golden Lake. Toward its end, you spoke of surrendering, saying something to the effect of, "Awakening arises when we can simply live our lives in a deep state of relaxation." That really resonated with me. Then, I juxtapose this idea of going out and living my life to the fullest and following my bliss, which is a very commonly shared piece of advice by some of the wisest authors and channels I've ever learned from: choose happiness and go where it feels good to go. So, now I'm challenged with fostering a deep sense of relaxation when I also feel I ought to get out and have more fun! These seem contradictory. Can you perhaps create a bridge between allowing integration to begin through deep relaxation versus living life to the fullest?*

Why does it have to be one or the other? Of course, you live in a physical reality that is to some degree an expression of duality. Because of this duality, there is going to be a sine wave of energies, so to speak. There are going to be times of winter or of relaxation and inactivity, and then there will be times of more activity and excitement. That is natural for a physical being. Just feel and honor your cycles. We don't see those two as contradictory. The paradox is that, in fourth density, you can actually experience the deepest state of relaxation when you are following your excitement, because you are in the flow instead of trying to create a flow. The third density egoic definition of excitement is very different than the fourth density one.

*That makes sense, and yes, of course, we can do both at the same time.*

*Please, forgive my impatience, which I suspect is common within third density. But if, as you say, it took thirteen thousand years for our winter to pass, will it take thirteen thousand years (and countless lifetimes) for us to successfully "do the work"? I want to see this done in a single lifetime! Is that realistic? Of course, it's going to be up to me. But when do the dividends get paid?*

The dividends are always being paid in the here and now, if you're willing to see them.

Remember, when evolution is viewed through the eyes of the ego, it's never fast enough. So, as you do this work that we've been talking about and you move out of the egoic "doing" orientation, you will go more into following the joy, which is the state of relaxation. Now, can you bring this idea of moving from a place of joy/relaxation during the times you are rushing to get something done? We know that it looks like they are contradictory. But if you can allow yourself to hold that feeling of relaxation *amidst* the feeling of being in a rush, it creates a paradoxical energy. And if you can find the midpoint between those two states, everything changes. That is inner alchemy.

---

*Yes, I can feel that.*

*This brings another question to mind, which might make you laugh: how to bypass the pain. Not because I don't want to feel it, but because it's not showing up! I know that Seth said, in a Jane Roberts book, that if someone has a blockage, an invisible limiting belief, and through self-reflection they're able to actually pinpoint that belief, then in that moment there will be a spontaneous transcending of the blockage. In some cases, their blockage might not be consciously identified, as I think you were alluding to, yet suddenly, through grasping greater truths, there will be an ease and a grace and a breakthrough that was not possible before.*

*And paraphrasing what Ramtha said in* The White Book, *channeled by J. Z. Knight, of his enlightenment long ago in Atlantean times, "If an ignorant buffoon like me, who could hack and kill and murder on his way to enlightenment, can do it, you can do it!" Meaning, if from the depths of ignorance, total separation and duality, there can be a moment of realization, where suddenly there is total clarity and a deep understanding of reality, then it hardly seems "inner work" is required.*

*Similarly, to build my case, there's the story of Saul in the Bible. He had set out to conquer the prophet Jesus and lay waste to his disciples, when suddenly, walking on the road to Damascus, he had this moment of spontaneous illumination that transformed him entirely.*

*So, with my desire and the examples gleaned from these passages, is there a way to bypass the healing work and move into a moment of spontaneous illumination?*

How can a "spontaneous" moment of illumination be something that you do or plan?

We don't want to go off on a nerdy history rant, but so many of your galactic ancestors have attempted to bypass their lessons over and over and over again, and not one could bypass anything; *they had to pass through.*

So, when you're talking about Seth's idea, that a momentary recognition of a belief system can totally shift things, that's absolutely true. That can happen. However, recognize that often those types of realizations are layered. This means that when you have one, it's only one layer that is removed, and the other layer might not show up for a year, for five years, or for three lifetimes. Or maybe the layer leading to a great transformation was preceded by many other previous layers peeling away that each had a less noticeable impact on the person, making it seem that the later layer accounted for the entire shift.

You used a very important word. You used the word *spontaneous.* Spontaneous means you can't control it. Therefore, if you can't control it, you can't charge through with your sword, forcing it to arrive. Then what do you do? You must simply be present in the moment and allow what arises, because that's the only way of passing through. Nothing exists but this present moment. If you allow the ego to continually focus on the future (as in "when" something will happen), you've taken yourself out of the here and now, which is the only place illumination is experienced. It is a conundrum, yes?

Back to relaxation. We're kind of laughing a little bit because it's almost as if we are picking up from you that, somehow, you did something wrong because you can't find your pain.

Nothing is wrong. If it hasn't arisen, it hasn't arisen for a reason. The reason it is hidden is not as important as honoring yourself in the here and now. Maybe there's nothing left for you to work with in this life. Maybe you haven't learned to recognize your pain that has hidden in plain sight. Who knows? This is why it's important not to keep trying to dig or else the act of digging becomes your spiritual practice. Then you end up digging a bunch of little shallow holes.

---

*In some of the things I've read and heard in my seeking, it almost sounds as if there's an internal mechanism, like an approval mechanism, that decides when you're ready for integration. I remember Seth saying something to the effect that if you were to abuse your ability of "remote viewing" because you wanted to spy on your neighbor, you would not be permitted—it would be blocked; it wouldn't work. You must have a completeness, which I presume includes a love and respect for all others, born from understanding and realization, or those faculties wouldn't be "given" to you.*

*Is there any kind of internal or external guard, guide, or judge who says you're ready or not ready, or is it a confluence of all your energies and wisdom that would make the illumination happen when you least expect it?*

Since we've already established that you all are that One hologram, then there's nobody outside of you to give approval. If we had to choose from the two choices you gave us, it would be the second one. It is a confluence of energies, impossible to plot on a graph, that has to do with your frequency.

When there is an alignment with a flow, then it takes you to the thing that you need.

If there is no alignment in the flow, such as me calling a pink elephant to walk in right now (and it doesn't), then the energy alignment is not there. It's a combination of a lot of different things that are beyond the mind's ability to track. Therefore, it brings us right back to the only place you can experience integration: here and now, in this moment.

*"I've recently heard that the soul of Vladimir Putin is Pleiadian and that his agenda is in sync with the Pleiadians, meaning what he is doing in Ukraine and elsewhere is not as negative as it seems. What is your view on that, Sasha?*

We must say, with all due respect, that we don't deal with interplanetary gossip! Being preoccupied with whose agenda is "good" and whose is "bad" only deepens the attachment to polarity. The Universe is infinitely wise and always in balance, even if the mind cannot see it or doesn't want to accept it. You're going to find that you'll have to release polarized thought in order to experience the integration process. As you shift more deeply into fourth density, you'll have very little interest in looking at outer events like this, because you'll have unshakable trust in the One to unfold whatever events are necessary in the larger landscape of balance.

*"If you're dealing with being overweight as a buffer from abuse, how would you talk or breathe into this?"*

We assume the questioner is asking this because being overweight does not have an obvious target point to use in the exercise we recommended. In that case, we suggest that you sit, quiet yourself, and try to bring up the trigger—not the full-on trauma trigger but a little trigger is okay. Bring up the trigger emotionally, and then ask yourself, "Where do I feel this in my body?"

It might be an obvious place, or it might be a very random place like your shoulder or something. It might be in the body, or it might even be an energetic spot away from the body. The energetic spots away from the surface of the body require a slightly more advanced way to work with it. If this is the case, and you're comfortable finding an energetic spot as opposed to a physical spot, you can work with it the same way.

To summarize, slightly trigger yourself when you've gotten into a quiet space, notice where you might feel that on your body or in your energy field, and then use that as the spot to breathe and work. Know that over time, this location may change. If so, follow where you feel guided to move.

---

*"How is the Pleiadian energy different or unique compared to Earth energy? How can we learn more about our own star family origins?"*

---

You know we love this topic. We could talk for two hours on it. So, let us see how we're going to approach your answer briefly...

We have presented a lot of work about the emotional wounds of the galactic family because as a species, we, too, had third density experiences. This means that we also had pain we eventually worked through on the species level.

One of the differences between us as species, even though we're very, very close, is that we Pleiadians have had a more natural, child-like curiosity. As a young species, we had a weakness to act when we shouldn't act, even with loving intentions. This has gotten us into trouble, creating some of our wounds. So, one of the differences in personality is that we are less cautious in some ways than humans. You may even label us a bit naïve when we were young because of our fondness to rush into situations spontaneously.

Third density is all about protection and survival. Fourth density is all about vulnerability. As Pleiadians, we had to work through our biggest fear when we were young, which was our fear of negativity. This included doing any kind of inner or shadow work. You have that fear too, though there are other things mixed in with that. Because we avoided and ignored our shadows as a third-density species, we had to face all of that when we entered fourth density. This repeated avoidance built a suppressed energy within us that came out in the form of a plague. That plague, which no medicine could cure, forced us to turn inward. We had to learn to embrace our shadow. It was very, very, very difficult, but it was the key that caused us to really pass through that dark night of the soul as a species and to awaken ourselves as we moved into fourth density.

Generally speaking, there are two main civilizations right now that are really helping you go through your transition. They are the Pleiadians and the Sirians. It is because we are so close to you, not only genetically but emotionally and ancestrally, that we can help you move through your difficult challenges.

There are so many ways to learn about your personal star family origins. The first is, as you become educated in the various galactic family lineages, to pay attention to your feelings of familiarity. As you also learn about some of their wounds (written about in *The Golden Lake*), you may see a parallel with your own challenges as a human, which is a big hint for you. We receive this question so often, and it is one of the reasons why the *Galactic Heritage Cards* were created—not simply to discover superficial information about star origins but to help heal the unfinished business and wounds brought to Earth from other lives in the stars.

We know that does not totally address your question because there's just too much there for a short answer, but hopefully that's helpful.

---

*You wrote in your book* The Golden Lake *about the bubbling up of joy in your world that's literally felt all the time. It's a constant state of euphoria. And I think you said that some of us have experienced that on Earth. You asked your readers, "Can you imagine feeling this constantly, all the time?"*

*Is that the reward? Is that where you still are right now—experiencing euphoria all the time? Or do you still battle your own "lions and tigers and bears"?*

We don't really battle them in the same way that we did in our past and the way you do now. Think of it this way: when you're carrying that heavy suitcase filled with stuff, you don't have a lot of energy for joy. Imagine that my civilization (or any fourth-density civilization) has gone through the process of unpacking our suitcases, passed through our challenges, and burned our burdens in a metaphorical transformational fire. What is left? Lightness. We are no longer carrying anything heavy. So, what's there not to be joyful about? Recognize, too, that from an old third-density perspective that's still polarized; euphoria and pain seem to be at opposite ends of the spectrum. To us, they have merged. Even pain can be beautiful and bittersweet when there are no more suitcases.

Our "euphoria" isn't like an ungrounded or polarized state. It's a state of complete integration. It's just *life* to us. It can be for you too.

That is what you're moving toward. But right now, you're still dealing with the suitcase. On the other end of your journey, yes, it is a very, very different, joyful, loving experience. Even the word *love* doesn't fully describe that state of consciousness.

---

*"Does your civilization also have angels or ascended masters?*

*Do archangels Michael and Gabriel also work with the Pleiadians?"*

What an interesting question. Thank you. When we went through our very difficult dark night of the soul as a species, the only way through was to reach out to the higher consciousnesses. Of course, they go by different names, but the universal archetypes are the same.

When our civilization went through those very dark times, we reached out to those higher beings—fifth density, sixth density—to really light the way through the tunnel for us. This is an important part of the evolution of any civilization.

---

*They were to you as perhaps you are to us?*

---

In some ways, yes—and as you will be to others.

*Why are you often over the country of Japan, as you stated earlier? What is the connection with this earthly location?*

This connection has to do with the deeper, inner agreements that Lyssa made for her work in this world. Because I am another incarnation of Lyssa, that commitment extends to me as well.

The reasons also have to do with the time period of your crossing thirteen thousand years ago when you went from summer into autumn, then into winter. We focus our energies there now to continue what was begun so long ago. We're not just there for the Japanese people but because Mount Fuji is a world energetic gateway, like an acupuncture point, that affects the entire planet. We're sometimes in other places as well.

*Can we ask for a demonstration? Is that too crude? Can you fire off some flares that make the news? Or individually, I've heard about [direct ET] contact and reaching out, some of which I learned from you.*

Those types of demonstrations are not really part of our agreement—to provide entertainment or validation. In addition, we have learned that no matter what "proof" we may give, it is often invalidated. From the many generations of contact programs my people have managed, we have learned that the best and easiest way to approach it is to help expand consciousness as a foundational step. When that happens, contact unfolds naturally because it is indeed a natural process. Many of you listening to this broadcast or reading these words have already felt your ET family reach out to you. You can always ask for contact. It all depends on the flow, the energy, and your personal agreements. Each of you already has your own team that works with you, and we do not interfere with your path. However, it is exciting when our paths do cross!

*"Why would anyone want to experience the lower-level densities when it's all pain and suffering? Is that the only way to realize the Oneness? If we came from this so-called Oneness, what is the point of leaving it?"*

Our answer will probably not be satisfactory, even if it is the truth. Why do you go on the most dangerous rollercoaster? Why do you dive with sharks? You do so purely for the experience. In that state of Oneness there is a stillness that does not allow consciousness to see itself. Only through the illusion of deep separation can consciousness see itself. After all, you cannot see your own face without a mirror.

From the egoic point of view, of course, it's very painful. But if you look at it from the larger point of view, it makes a lot of sense.

*I don't know that I could add to what you're saying, but I believe that 99 percent of the time, a person's life is not all pain and all suffering. Even through our pain and suffering, most of us still feel our lives are laced with beauty and love. I trust that, to some degree or another, virtually all lifetimes experience this.*

Yes. You must remember that the sun, like the light of your being, still exists even when there's a cloudy sky. Part of any painful experience is the option to remember your true nature and reunite with the sun. You simply have to pass through the clouds in order to do so. It may be unimaginable now but, as you evolve, pain and joy merge into a very rich, profound experience.

*Brilliant! I don't think I can convey how privileged I feel for having experienced your wisdom, Sasha and Lyssa. Thank you so very much. Your insights are extraordinary, and they touch me and my heart very deeply. Any final words?*

We simply want to remind all of you *how deeply you are loved.* That is what it comes down to. Since there is no one outside of you, ultimately there is only Oneness. You may feel separated from it, but your awakening comes as you remember it and learn to love yourselves. In doing so, you will also remember (and deeply experience) how much you are loved by all of creation. When you're in physical reality, the experience of loving yourself becomes the hardest thing to learn. But it is the most necessary step on the path that will help you shift through the gateway into fourth density so that you can remember your true nature and return to that love. It has not disappeared. It's just a little obscured right now, like clouds obscure the sun.

---

*To find out more about Lyssa, her books, and Sasha please visit Lyssa's website at www.lyssaroyal.net.*

# Chapter 2

## Tapping into Your True Power
## *with Salvatore Rachele*

### About Sal

Sal is a teacher, healer, mystic, and priest with more than forty-five years of experience in the human potential movement. He's the author of *The Secrets of Unlimited Energy, The Mystery of Time, The Real History of Earth, Soul Integration, Life on the Cutting Edge,* and *Earth Awakens*—the extraordinary insights and wisdom within each reveals Sal and his guides to be true pioneers of consciousness. He also conducts workshops and seminars all over the world on the topics of healing and ascension. And as an accomplished pianist, he's composed several recordings of original meditative music.

In these pages, Sal will be channeling his spirit guides, The Founders. They're a group of twelfth-dimension beings of pure light, appearing to Sal as bright blue-white stars. They've been helping humanity for as long as we've graced the face of the Earth, which is for far longer than mainstream science now tells us.

Today's information is about how to be empowered and, specifically, how to express your powerful spiritual nature in the world. The Founders are going to share specific steps we can take to manifest our spiritual power on this human plane.

*Welcome, Sal! Let's bring on The Founders.*

---

Greetings, dear creators. We are The Founders. It's our pleasure and privilege to be with you. It's always our delightful challenge to present our material in a way that is basic enough for everyone to understand, yet advanced enough to challenge and push you forward a little bit on your path.

That is our intention today. We will stay very brief and simple, allowing more time for complexities during our Q and A section. Our presentation may feel as though it's a mere review for some of you, but we know this is important for the wider audience this material will ultimately reach. Grasping the basic metaphysical truths of your existence is absolutely fundamental in your ultimate self-realization. Regardless, we're here together—our group, this channel, and all of you—for one purpose, and that is to grow: to expand awareness, to expand consciousness, to ascend into higher frequencies of understanding, and to be empowered.

## Tapping into Your True Power

The word *power* is a little bit of a dirty word in some spiritual circles. Many of you were brought up with the Christian concept of the meek inheriting the Earth. Keep in mind, however, that the Bible has been translated through many different languages, and its original meanings are sometimes lost or clouded.

*Meek*, at the time it was used in the Bible, meant humble. Humble means being willing to learn as a child would learn, with childlike wonder and curiosity. It does not mean being subservient. It does not mean being a doormat that other souls will trample over, forcing their will upon you. This has been a major misunderstanding, resulting in a lot of souls who feel guilty if they even think about being powerful.

There is not a problem, however, with true power. Consider: true power comes from God, and the kingdom of God lies within you. You are all-powerful, creative, spiritual beings, which bears repeating as a mantra, said in first person:

*I am a powerful, creative, spiritual being.*

That is an accurate statement, as true as any words can possibly be since your true identity is beyond all words.

Words are just descriptions. They point at the truth; they are not the actual truth. The word *tree* is not the actual thing being described. When we say *tree*, you form an image in your mind of what a tree looks like, with branches and roots and leaves and so on. But the word *tree* is obviously not the tree. So, the word *truth* is not the truth. It is a word that points you to the truth. In this case, the truth is you are infinitely powerful.

Now, you may say, "Well, I don't feel infinitely powerful. I've got problems in my marriage or problems with my business and finance (or problems with my health or some other problem), and I don't feel very powerful right now." That doesn't mean you're not powerful; it means you're experiencing your power in a way that seems to be disempowering.

Why is that? Because some part of you *believes* you are powerless or that you have very limited power. What most don't realize is that your beliefs are so powerful, you can experience feeling powerless simply because *you believe* you are powerless, which actually proves that you are powerful. So powerful that you can imagine yourself to be unlike your creator, even though you were created in the image and likeness of your creator.

Take a moment to just breathe deeply, taking in what we just said. Next, we're going to give you a simple process for reclaiming, remembering, and standing in your power.

## Reclaiming Your Power

First, let us differentiate between true power and false power. Unlike what we've just shared, false power is what you mostly see when you look around the world today.

There's a group of souls, maybe a few hundred or a few thousand in number, who think of themselves as the power elite. Outsiders have called them the Illuminati, the Cabal, or the Powers That Be. We say with absolute certainty, these souls have what is called false power. They are not in their true power.

Ask yourself a basic question: If you were truly in your power, aware of the Kingdom of God within you radiating forth from the center of your being out into the world, would you have a need to control and manipulate other human beings? Would you have a desire to oppress or enslave others? To force your ideologies upon them? Of course not. Any being who feels such a need to forcefully control other beings is operating from false power.

True power comes from within. And if you're in your power, you'd have absolutely no desire to control other human beings, nor would you ever see them as a threat to you. You'd no longer be driven by fear but by the divine power within you. This is not a mental concept but an energetic reality.

We encourage all of you right now to breathe deeply and feel the meaning behind our words. Don't just intellectually digest these words as a nice idea. Instead, this is about feeling the energy of what we say at a deep level within your being when we acknowledge your inner divine power.

## Remembering Your Power

Let's go through some steps you can take to manifest your God-given divine power on this Earth. The very first thing you must do is let go of the core negative belief that you are powerless. Perhaps you think that you're just one little human in a vast sea of humanity, unheard by your government, church, or medical community. Or you think that you have just one vote, if that, in a broken political system, a pawn in some power elite's chess game.

We invite you right now to let go of this core negative belief that you are powerless. We already explained it's not so. Your life has already proven it's not so. You are a powerful, creative, spiritual being.

Your spiritual nature is also easy to prove using mainstream physics. If you recall, the light spectrum and the sound spectrum make up narrow little bands. Lights exists between infrared and ultraviolet, and audio exists between ultra-low frequency and high frequency sounds. All your physical experiences of sight and sound exist in these tiny, little, narrow bands, while the spiritual universe, by any definition, is far vaster than what your physical senses perceive.

You vibrate in the infrared and ultraviolet spectrum, but you also vibrate in many, many levels and dimensions besides these narrow little physical bands. You are spiritual. Every moment of every day that you are creating, your existence extends far beyond simply detecting light and audio. And your power to create is exactly what this workshop is about—the creative adventure of who you are and the awakening adventure of who you are. By awakening, we mean becoming aware of who you really are right now.

Enlightenment is not somewhere in the future after you say enough mantras or do enough meditations or go to enough gurus or sit in enough ashrams. Enlightenment is now. Now is the only place enlightenment can possibly exist. You are therefore enlightened right now, just as you are powerful right now.

Just as most of you are unaware of your power in this very moment, so are you unaware of your enlightenment. Neither are something to attain but merely to realize. You need to realize the nature of your true self as a child of God—unlimited, creative, and powerful. You only need to realize these characteristics of yourself, and that's why "self-realization" is the most accurate term for enlightenment. You are now on a path of self-realization. You are finally discovering the truth of who you really are as a powerful, creative, spiritual being. This is an accurate statement of who and where you are, using words that are our best approximations.

You are here to realize your true self, as opposed to only knowing yourself as your ego. Ego is the false self that believes in false power. The ego believes in separation from God, and it identifies with your physical body, mind, and personality. Your ego thinks these make up who you are, which is why it's full of fear. It knows the body is easily assailed with weapons or natural disasters—being too hot, too cold, or whatever. By identifying with a physical form, you feel powerless and helpless. "Oh my God, what if Russia turns off the gas, and we all freeze this winter?" Some countries in Europe are thinking those thoughts right now. What if somebody declares war on us? What if we run out of money? What if this, what if that? All based on identifying with the little, human self.

At this moment on Earth, you are One expressing through billions. It is time to begin identifying with your true self, which is beyond time and space. It is infinite. It is omnipresent—everywhere present. You are a child of God. You are the offspring of the Creator of everything, and therefore, you are unlimited. You are infinite in your abilities, in your scope of awareness, and of all you can do, be, and have. You're here to expand your own awareness to become aware of your infinite possibilities for expression.

## Standing in Your Power

One of the ways to get in touch with your powers is to live primarily from your heart and solar plexus and less from your head. Some of you have already learned to go from your head to your heart. We're suggesting that's not the end of the story. The next step would be to go from your heart to your solar plexus, and then finding the right balance between there and your heart.

Your third eye is the center of wisdom, your heart is the center of love and compassion, and your solar plexus is the center of power. Ideally, then, you want wisdom, love, and power to all work together in order to create with the most effectiveness in the world. If all you do is come from your solar plexus—your power center—you become like a bulldozer running over people or like a bull in a china shop, devoid of wisdom and love.

Temper your power with love and care. Be compassionate toward other human beings. Tap into your own wisdom by considering the long-term consequences of your behaviors. Too few think, for example, of the long-term consequence of polluting your planet with plastic. Today, every life form on Earth is polluted by plastic to some degree. Fortunately, with wisdom and love, you're beginning to adapt; otherwise, you, as a species, would have been extinct by this time.

Look at the long-term consequences of your actions. That's where the wisdom component comes in. Having love for all life forms will guide you. Then you will come into your true power, in the solar plexus chakra. These are some of the steps to manifesting your power that will avoid the frequent scenario of things not turning out the way you planned.

## The Power of Rising Vibrations

Let's now compare individual will and collective will. Let's say you're in a room with one hundred people, and you believe in peace, but the other ninety-nine people believe in war. Your thoughts of peace will have a very strong impact on you—and they may influence many of the people in the room—but if all other things are equal, you're likely to have an inclination for war in that room of one hundred people.

Rarely, however, are all other things equal. Obviously, some of you have developed your power more than others, and this is where raising your vibration comes in—raising your vibration in consciousness as well as in your physical form. One of the best ways to do this is to be around other high- vibrational souls. Maybe spending time with teachers, yogis, sages, mystics, and people that perhaps have been working on themselves longer than you have. You can go to an ashram in India, watch a video of a Western teacher, or attend events such as this one where there's six different teachers, each one with a slightly different viewpoint or a different angle on reality. Then, you can synthesize the very best of each into your own internal wisdom, aligning with those parts that are beneficial to your soul growth, happiness, and well-being.

As you raise your vibration, you become more and more powerful and able to influence more and more people in the world. Now if you were to enter that same room of one hundred people as a more powerful being believing in peace and the ninety-nine others believing in war have not done the work on themselves—maybe just following mainstream media who is beating the drums of aggression and galvanizing people to be opposed to the evil in the world—your silent influence would dramatically increase. Pretty soon, even though you're one out of a hundred, you'd have a disproportionate share of the creative power, capable of neutralizing the energies of everyone else around you.

Suddenly, the score would be even. Now the war and peace equation is balanced, even though there's only one of you that believes in peace. You will have become almost one hundred times more powerful than those who believe in fear, war, and negativity.

Raising your own vibration is the best way to influence this world, which is as simple as working on yourself to tap into your own power. Combined with the compounding effect of your positive influence on the collective beliefs of others, you'll realize you can exponentially offset some of the negative beliefs on this planet. Come together with like-minded people who are also working on themselves, and you'll become a powerful force for good in the world. Ten of you will have the power of a thousand. Ten thousand will have the power of one million. Ten million will have the power of one billion. This is how it happens. This is how a planet shifts into higher frequencies.

Next, we'll look at how to further accelerate your own ascension by acknowledging your own fears, working with your breath, minimizing distractions, and curbing addictions.

## Working on Yourself

### *Moving through Fear*

So, how do you get to the place where you're manifesting your power, feeling powerful, and creating powerfully in the world? We need to go through the blockages together. All of us here, together, we're going to walk through the blockages to realizing your true power. And, of course, fear is one of the biggest blockages.

You live in a world that is dominated by fear. As this channel says, there is truly a pandemic on Earth. It could be called "fear-itis." Three-fourths or more of humanity is ruled by some sort of fear—whether over a virus, the government, church, possible disasters, poverty; almost everyone is afraid of something. Yet, to get to a place where you're creating powerfully in the world, you must take an honest assessment of yourself to remove any blockages of fear. How much fear do you have, where is it located in your consciousness, where does it arise, and how can you move through it? These blockages must be freed; they cannot be sidestepped or bypassed. You must move through your fears.

Once you're aware of the fear, notice what thoughts and concerns have triggered it. Ask yourself things like, "What is it I'm afraid of?" "How do I feel unsafe?" or "Why am I worried about my family being unsafe?" Find the fear in your body and observe how it's moving within you. You'll find there's a sensation, an energetic pattern moving through your body. Then breathe deeply.

Step one is identifying the fear. Step two is breathing deeply, which moves the energy.

### *Harnessing Your Breath*

Most of you have not learned how to breathe properly. If you master breathing, you'll have made giant strides toward raising your vibration into the ascension realms. Many of the yogis, including Babaji, reached their ascended state through breathing yoga—Kriya yoga in the case of Babaji. However, there's other forms of yoga, such as Kundalini yoga. There are many forms of breathing, such as rebirthing and primal therapy, that not only bring more oxygen into your blood and purify and cleanse your physical body but also move emotions so you don't stay stuck in your fear and the incessant worry it can trigger.

Breathing deeply and staying present in the moment as the fear moves through your body is the beginning of the undoing of fear.

When you're breathing, notice the details of your fear. Does it have a color? A flavor? A texture? What might it look like, sound like, or taste like? Pay great attention and stay aware of these details. Finally, ask your Higher Self, the all-wise part of you that exists right now within, to move you through the fear. Essentially, you're asking your Higher Self to take it over, to take charge of the fear, and move it in whatever way your Higher Self deems appropriate.

But first, you have to stay present with it. Stay present and then breathe. Notice the details of it. Identify the thoughts that generate it. Then ask your Higher Self to remove it. In that order.

### *Minimizing Distractions*

You live in a world that worships fear, and you live in a world of constant distractions. The number one distraction is the belief that you need things from outside of yourself to be whole and complete.

Your mainstream television and all their commercials want you to believe you *need* this product or that service to be more sexy, beautiful, healthy, prosperous, or whatever. That's how your system works. People often buy products because they think they're lacking in some way. They're too easily convinced that they need to fill up their life with lots of unimportant things to feel good about themselves.

You need only become aware of all distractions that take you out of your center, where your true power resides. Stop trying to be or think like the celebrities you admire or idolize, thinking that they somehow have a power, quality, or charm you're missing. You're already your own magnificent creation, unlike any other. You were born worthy of all your heart's desires. And you are good enough, just the way you already are, to live an abundantly happy life.

### *Curbing Addictions*

Next, be honest with yourself, noticing any bad habits or addictions you may have. In the Alcoholic Anonymous program, the first step is to admit that you have given your power over to alcohol. It may not be alcohol in your case. It could be an addiction to some hobby or pastime that's gone beyond simply enjoying yourself into being addictive, such as TV, video games, food, or drugs, obviously. Or it might be a little more subtle, such as being addicted to thinking.

Yes, that's a big one: being addicted to thinking. Being addicted to your rational, logical mind. Being addicted to your ego and allowing your ego and your rational mind to run your life because you're afraid of letting go and experiencing what the ego would perceive as emptiness, even though there is no such thing. Letting go of one source of stimuli opens you up to others.

The ego will do anything to fill up your days with mindless activity rather than face its own fear of death—its own fear of nothingness. You must not be afraid to be alone in silence, to slow down and detach from your daily drama, whether it's twenty minutes twice a day or doing some breathing or yoga in the morning and maybe again a little bit in the evening before you go to bed.

Then look for the more subtle addictions, such as the addiction to judgment. Maybe you've learned not to judge others but you're still judging yourself. Or there's the addiction to labeling or to being right or to being unhappy.

It's absolutely necessary to look within and do the work on yourself. There's no shortcut. Just saying a couple affirmations won't cut it when every day you're bombarded with negativity and fear from those still afraid.

Do not be afraid of being powerful.

---

*My first questions are based on your 2013 book* Soul Integration.

*You wrote: "Now that Earth is ascending in vibration, it will become easier for souls to demonstrate the immortality available to the physical body. In the next thirty to forty years, a large number of souls will go through physical ascension."*

*Is this happening now? How many souls? And is getting to that place of ascension simply a matter of unleashing your power with some of your named steps, such as facing fear and breathing through it?*

---

Well, you could say we have both good news and not so good news regarding the topic of ascension and, specifically, building the immortal crystal light body. The good news is, yes, the program is still happening. Everything is moving forward in the proper steps for this physical ascension to take place on Earth. However, free will planets such as Earth have variable timeframes. There's a reason it's taking longer than originally predicted for physical ascension to take place on Earth, and it all comes back to being powerful, creative, spiritual beings.

Here's the other part—the not so good news. Those souls who are creating negatively are also powerful, creative, spiritual beings. Now, we just went through an example where you can raise your vibration to the point where you offset the negative souls. Nevertheless, these are still powerful beings creating negatively.

There's been a lot of negativity on Earth for a very long time, and it's taking a little longer than originally planned to offset. The ascension is still happening, though the timetable has shifted—not by a great deal from our perspective. There's about a ten-to-fifteen-year delay on the original plan; the first wave of ascension was originally going to happen around 2030, and now, we're looking at maybe 2040.

*So, energetic changes are now happening on Planet Earth. I would imagine in my naïveté —which is why I'm asking you—that the energy is irrevocably rising, and whether or not we surf that wave is the question. Is that right? Or has the fear slowed down the planet's rate of increased vibrations?*

Well, the planet herself continues to raise in vibration. What happens is, as some souls become more and more out of phase with the natural ambient state of their planet, they start to have what has been termed immune system failure. This is all before COVID-19 came into the picture, yet COVID-19 is one of the ways in which the immune system can be compromised. It's been written that there will seem to be exotic new viruses showing up in the world creating pandemics and things like that when, in reality, there have always been more than 150 viruses in the average human body. Right now, your bodies have at least 150 different viruses in them, so why are you not constantly sick? Because of your immune system.

But the immune system becomes compromised by many factors, including GMOs, plastics, electromagnetic radiation, and industrial pollution, although the biggest one of all is core negative thoughts, primarily fear. So, you have approximately three-fourths of humanity dominated by fear, damaging their immune systems.

Now, you have some souls who took vaccines, and they believed the vaccines would make them better, and because of the power of belief, some of them did improve through the use of vaccines. The problem is, many souls on Earth may superficially believe that they're doing something positive for their bodies, but at a deeper level, they have their unacknowledged subconscious fears. And those fears mingle with the idea that vaccines are going to hurt the body rather than help it. It's the same thing with different viruses, bacteria, chemical weapons, biological weapons, etcetera.

---

*Okay. I believe—and I'm looking for your confirmation—that anybody reading this who is aware of, or interested in, reclaiming their power can choose to move in that direction, to be a light, a bringer of the dawn, and raise their vibration to any degree they permit themselves to through knowledge and wisdom, correct?*

That is correct. Every soul is created equal from a certain way of looking at it, although every soul is also unique and different at the same time. And since all of you are created in the image and likeness of God, all of you are capable of creating like God creates. You can each create an entire universe once you reach a certain level of consciousness, which is considerably beyond where most of you are at the present time.

*Another favorite passage of mine in your book* Soul Integration: *"Once a soul has progressed to a high level of integration, psychic and spiritual powers are a natural byproduct of such levels of awareness. You do not need to seek them out. They come to you."*

*You also wrote: "Ascension is a normal, natural process once a soul has reached a certain level of awareness."*

*Twice, then, you wrote about a certain "level of awareness." Can you speak to the level of awareness you're referring to and the interplay with soul integration? What is soul integration?*

Well, soul integration is bringing together the various parts of the soul into a cohesive whole so that all your parts are functioning with efficiency. There are six lower bodies that are part of soul integration. Three of them are well known—the physical, emotional, and mental. And then you have the three subtle bodies, which are the astral, etheric, and causal.

You all have these six lower bodies, and they all need to be aligned, working together in cooperation, to create soul integration. Once you have your six lower bodies working together, then it's possible to truly manifest your power, and you find that you're influencing larger numbers of souls just by your intention.

Once a soul is integrated, your Higher Self, comprised of six *higher* bodies—the soul, the oversoul, the monad, and three God levels above the monad, comprising levels seven through twelve—is able to permeate your six lower bodies because they're all lined up. Think of your higher bodies as the shackles on a key and your lower bodies like the tumblers in a padlock. When everything is lined up, you can open the lock, so to speak, which in this case means you can receive the Higher Self frequencies coming into your lower-level bodies.

This is what we mean by soul integration. As you integrate the soul, your vibration naturally rises to the point where you're no longer affected by the negative influences and problems that are occurring on the planet. Then it's possible to be healthy all the time and to maintain an eternally youthful body.

In this channel's book *The Secrets of Unlimited Energy*, he goes into the science of immortality a little bit, which is very simple science that can be summed up as *energy in equals energy out.* If you take the dissipating factors that cause the physical body to grow old and die, and you balance them with the incoming energy factors (i.e., regenerative factors), you can achieve an equilibrium where the body is no longer aging, growing old, and dying. To do this, you open to higher frequencies that are not bound by what is called the Law of Entropy or the Law of Decay or the Law of Chaos or the Second Law of Thermodynamics—there are many words to describe this—which is exclusively in the domain of the lower dimensions.

In such an equilibrium, you can literally ascend into higher frequencies, gaining those powers that you were talking about earlier—teleportation, bilocation, telekinesis, and psychokinesis, which are the abilities to influence material things with your mind. Those abilities are not just given to any soul that wants them, because they inherently possess the potential for violating the free will of others.

You've heard the expression "faith can move mountains." Could you imagine having the power to actually move a mountain? What if there are ten thousand people living on the side of that mountain, and they don't want you moving it? You can see the types of free will conflicts that may arise from having that level of power available to you.

---

*That's the power that's innately within all of us! And, as I'm beginning to understand, with the rising vibrations now at play on planet Earth, we're able to do the work—to face our fears—as we move to master self in a far more efficient, easier, and quicker way than ever before, allowing us to access those powers within ourselves, contingent on the constraint of our free not will interfering with that of others.*

Yes. And, of course, you've probably heard of the book *A Course in Miracles*. There are many ways to perform so-called miracles. Healings, for example: when somebody has two weeks to live—the cancer's all through their body—they receive a healing and two weeks later they're in perfect health instead of a grave. These types of healings happen frequently around the world with different healers. As we said, you all have the ability to move mountains. But as you raise your vibrations, you also raise your responsibility levels, and you begin to realize at a very deep level how and when to use your abilities wisely, for the true good of all involved (their true good, not your idea of what's best for them).

There are safeguards built into this universe, even though some may know of black magic practitioners who've used these abilities to hurt others. Such instances involve far more than meets the eye, so let us just say the universe works in perfect balance. Generally speaking, souls are not given these advanced abilities until they demonstrate a responsibility in how they'll use them.

---

*Twice now you've said "being given permission." Is there a permission mechanism? Is there a higher portion of ourselves that says, "Okay, Mike can go and do whatever he chooses?" Or is it more of a confluence of our own energies, our own love brought to bear, with a self-realization that makes it possible to move a mountain?*

It's a combination of both of those qualities. This is a situation where you have a realization of how you interact with the other forces in the universe, the idea of the one in the many, *e pluribus unum* as you say in your Latin, "out of many, one." You have the groups and subgroups of humanity that are aligned in different belief systems, who are creating miniature realities within the larger reality, and then you have, of course, the individuals. One of the tasks we have as higher-dimensional beings is to examine the effects of free will exercised by one group upon another.

Let's use an example. Let's say that there's a group of manipulative forces who want to enslave others using artificial intelligence, nanobots, and other technological methods. If we as a group of higher dimensional entities were to prevent such enslavement, we'd be interfering with the free will of those negative energies by counteracting their desire to influence the masses. Similarly, if we were to allow the manipulative forces to have their way, this would impact the free will of those who do not want to be enslaved. So, it can be a rather intricate and complex dance of collective free wills that, if otherwise left to play itself out, would ultimately, perhaps over thousands of years, find its own balance anyway.

*You're speaking of your own involvement in the affairs of Earth, for which you've implied there's always some degree of subjectivity?*

Even though we are at what you would call a high dimension, in assisting you we're still dealing with a free will planet. It's therefore not our intention to interfere with this any more than absolutely necessary. But once you reach a critical mass of souls who wish to break free of limitation, then we are allowed to intervene in very specific ways.

Now, there's another group, which many of you have heard of, that some call the Galactic Federation or Galactic Confederation. That particular group has been tasked with making sure you do not blow yourselves up with nuclear weapons. So they have, on several occasions, intervened directly in your nuclear weapons programs, which seems to contradict what we may call the non-interference principle, and yet it would have violated the free will of a large number of souls if a nuclear war were allowed on the Earth.

There's also a group of souls some call the Karmic Guardians who actually do the day-to-day determination of what is allowed and what is not allowed from the point of view of free will and pre-destiny. This is many thousands of souls that are assigned to different regions of the Earth, and their task is to uphold the principles of free will and pre-destiny as they are delineated by the Godhead.

*Quoting again from your book Soul Integration: "Ecstasy and bliss do not happen in the unknowable. They happen when we return from our journey and enter back into the world. The unknowable is the void. But something happens in the void, something we cannot explain, and when we return, it is entirely possible to be filled with God's limitless love and compassion. We return to the world gladly because we are free of it, even as we notice that we still have a body, mind, and personality."*

*In Soul Integration, you also quoted the book A Course in Miracles, "the last step in the reawakening of knowledge is taken by God," which I expect means souls can be brought and taught (like you're teaching us right now) how to find their power, face their fears, and move through them. You can take us up to the brink, but then it's up to—and here it says God—to decide when we can cross that threshold and tap into infinite wisdom. Again, it's indicated God decides. I know words can fail when applied to truth; the word "tree" is not a tree, as you said earlier.*

*What can you say about this "point" in each of our private journeys, in which we move from not knowing to knowing or from unrealized into realized?*

Let us remind you again of the limitation of words. In *A Course in Miracles*, the word *knowledge* is interchangeable with the word *enlightenment*, and the word *perception* has more to do with what most people call *knowledge*. So, we're dealing with the words *God* and *Godhead*, the word *source*, the words *knowable* and *unknowable*, and the words the void, which is beyond what can be known. These are all aspects of what could be called God.

Then there are two definitions of God, which are used interchangeably in most spiritual teachings. One is more accurately referred to as the Godhead, or the source of the radiant energy that emanates out of the void into the manifest creation. That Godhead is an eternal, unchanging source that has a continually changing radiation of energy and love emanating from it. You could also say that God is everything that is and what's beyond everything that is—it includes everything.

If you use those definitions, then you can also talk about the knowable and unknowable aspects of God. When we say unknowable, we mean there is no recording device such as a mind that's sitting there saying, "I'm having an enlightenment experience and God looks like this and God is this big and this small." None of that is happening in the unknowable aspect of God because it is unknowable. It is not something that can be comprehended with the mind, as it is known. There is no recall where you can say, "Well, when I went into the Godhead, there were these twenty-four thrones or elders of the throne, and they did this and they did that, and then they took me here and they took me there."

No. There may be a realm like that which you can recall—that would be the knowable aspect of God. But there would be a realm beyond that, that cannot be known or described by the mental consciousness.

---

*Yes. That's masterfully described, as are the words you chose in the book. The distinction I'd like to focus on is when it's said that God decides the last step toward enlightenment. Individually, it seems, we can bring ourselves only up to a certain point with preparation, but what is that spark of God that says, "You're now realized"? Can you describe that?*

Well, you have in the Eastern traditions what's called Samadhi and Mahasamadhi. Samadhi is attained when you can remove from your mind all confusion, illusions, and barriers, leaving you in a state of continuous awareness of your oneness with God—a state of enlightenment. Then you have Mahasamadhi for which there is no path. The idea "God will take the final step" is simply another way of saying there's nothing you as an individual can do to attain Mahasamadhi, or this unknowable state of supreme enlightenment. You can reach the state of Samadhi and basically say, "Okay, God, it's up to you if you want to take me further than this." Again, mere words are not adequate, because they further imply time and space. It's not about further or nearer or any of those words that are part of a limited reality.

But there is a reality beyond Samadhi, a reality beyond knowing that you're one with God. That's as much as we can say using your language.

---

*You also wrote of another fascinating paradox: "The last thing to be given up is the desire for enlightenment. Until you reach that point, your one burning desire is to be free of Maya, Lila[4], or whatever you call it, and to embrace the Divine. This may become an all-consuming obsession, perhaps the only obsession worth having.*

*"The very act of trying to attain something negates enlightenment. As one Zen master said, 'Enlightenment is not what you think.' Therefore, we must go beyond the mind in order for enlightenment to dawn on us."*

*Can you please address this paradox where enlightenment may be the only obsession worth having yet the obsession itself actually negates enlightenment?*

It's the greatest paradox, because you're already enlightened and yet you have this belief that enlightenment is somewhere in the past or future. Maybe you have a distant memory of being enlightened at some point, and then you descended into these lower worlds where you became addicted or hypnotized by the illusions. Or you have this idea that at some far point in the future, after doing enough mantras or yoga or meditation or sitting at the feet of enough gurus, you'll somehow become enlightened once again.

That is the perception of an unenlightened soul. When you are enlightened, you realize you have always been enlightened and always will be enlightened—where there was perhaps a moment when you blinked your eyes and some other state of consciousness

[4]Both Maya and Lila refer to the hypnotic grip of life's illusions and dramas upon our conscious focus.

happened for just a split second in between always being enlightened. And, of course, in that twinkling of an eye went millions of years of incarnating into lower worlds and trying to attain some state of enlightenment.

Enlightenment deals with the timeless and the desireless realms. The desire to be in a state of no desire. We don't mean a resignation, dullness, or "nothing appeals to me, I'm just going to be bored" state. Enlightened "desireless-ness" means you recognize you already have everything and there's nothing to desire. It's a timeless state, because once you're no longer desiring something, you're no longer projecting anything into the future. You realize that everything is in the present; everything is now. You come to a total acceptance of the now.

There are many Eastern teachers who talk about this state of total acceptance, where there is no resistance to what is. That means being in complete peace with what is—including war, poverty, misery, and suffering. Whatever's going on in the world, you're in complete acceptance of it. It doesn't mean you approve of it, but you're not defining it as wrong in any way. You're in a state of complete nonjudgment. So, it's a desireless, nonjudgmental, non-dual state. There are many words others use to describe it.

---

*"As we step into this new phase of evolution, how will money be perceived? Will it lose all meaning or take on a different meaning altogether? What does this look like and how can we prepare for this?"*

Well, first of all, it's important to understand what money is. It's a tool like a hammer is a tool. It's neutral: not good or bad. You can build weapons with it or you can feed the poor with it, just as you can use a hammer to build a house or hit somebody over the head.

Money is neutral. It's a tool to make the trading of goods and services more convenient. It's not always convenient to take a wheelbarrow of apples to the marketplace to exchange for a wheelbarrow of oranges, especially because oranges get ripe about three months after apples do. So you've invented a symbol, which could be coin or paper with presidents' faces on it or whatever, as a convenient way of trading goods and services among a group of human beings.

That's all money is, but you've made it into a god and you've worshiped it. Of course, we're talking about humanity in general. Many have come to think their well-being depends on having a certain number of these pieces of paper or metal discs, and therefore, they spend an inordinate amount of time worrying about having enough.

You can see how it's evolved throughout your history, with all the wars that have been fought over economics, the creation of "haves and the have nots," and the immense imbalances that have occurred as a result of worshipping money as the object of your happiness instead of God and the unlimited forces of creation.

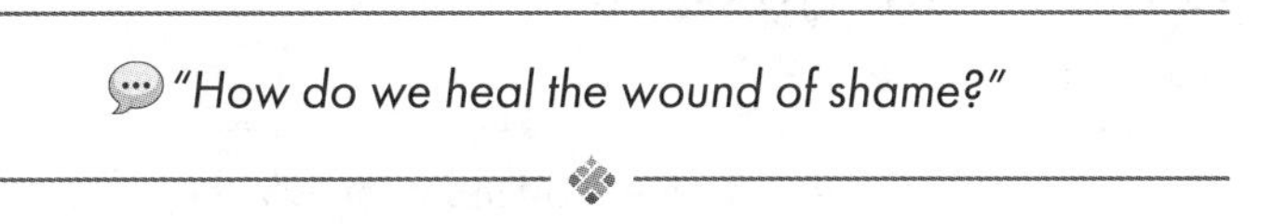
*"How do we heal the wound of shame?"*

Shame is an emotional component that is closely related to guilt, and it's based on the idea that you are inherently defective, you are a bad person deserving punishment, and you've done something unforgivable, and therefore, you're going to be condemned by other human beings or God.

It's a misunderstanding of who you are. Yes, there is a thing called conscience, which can be useful in guiding a soul that is relatively inexperienced—the baby soul or young soul—in learning which behaviors are lifting humanity and which behaviors are holding humanity back, i.e., interfering with spiritual growth. When you sense that you have done something to interfere in the growth of another person, you may feel an uncomfortable feeling, which we'll call conscience. But if it's taken internally to mean I'm a bad person because I interfered with this soul's free will, then it becomes guilt, and the resulting emotion of shame is derived from that.

*So, how do you heal it? How do you face it and breathe through it?*

You heal it by remembering who you are. By realizing that who you are is beyond judgment and condemnation. That who you are is a beautiful child of God. That you're inherently innocent at a spiritual level, even if you've behaved badly on the human plane.

You differentiate between human *behavior* and who you *are* as a spiritual being. Recognize that you are still an innocent child of God. Then you can forgive yourself for your bad behavior. Yes, you might want to make a promise that you will not repeat what you've done, but once the lesson is learned, there's no longer any reason you would.

You're like the child who didn't know the stove was hot, so you burned your hand on it. Now, if you keep touching it and keep burning your hand, then you've got a problem. However, learn from your mistakes, and you can forgive yourself and move on.

There's no need to ever experience shame.

---

*You've suggested that moment by moment, whether pursuing joy or avoiding pain or at a fork in the road of life, we ask ourselves, "What would my Higher Self do in this situation?" Can you speak to this?*

It sounds like a bit of Zen, and it's like the Hollywood advice, "fake it until you make it." You're pretending that you're coming from your Higher Self when maybe you're coming from ego. But it actually works because you *are* your Higher Self, and ultimately, the ego does not exist; it's an illusion. It arises from your belief in separation.

So, if you approach anything as if you were already the Higher Self, you're simply convincing the subconscious mind of what is already so. If you can get your subconscious mind to believe that you are the Higher Self, then it's going to say, "Okay, I *am* the Higher Self," and it will align with the Higher Self.

It works. It tricks the mind, but it works.

---

*You practice and administer "Timeline Healing." Will you briefly explain what it is?*

Timeline Healing is a very powerful therapy that this channel has experienced as being far more powerful than ordinary psychotherapy, and it involves time travel: going back in time to give past versions of yourself a healing.

It was directly brought to this channel by the Arcturians, although other techniques that are most similar are past-life regression, Theta Healing, hypnotherapy, and the Silva Method. Those interested in learning more can visit this channel's website (listed at the end of this chapter).

---

*Do other dimensions have an investment or an interest in us here on Earth elevating consciousness and awakening? Does it benefit them in some way too?*

Absolutely. For example, take the Arcturians, who come from the Arcturus star system and who are highly evolved beings. They have no karma with Earth. They're not here to make amends for something they did in the past. But they have a great love for humanity, and so they have been visiting you for a long time. They're the ones who are largely responsible for keeping major earthquakes and volcanoes away from heavily populated areas, with about a 96 percent success rate. They're very happy with the work they've been able to do to give humanity more time to get themselves together without having quite so many cataclysms.

This channel also has a group of Arcturians that do physical and etheric healing on many of the clients who have health problems. They care deeply about the future of humanity, while also respecting free will, and so they only intervene in limited ways. For balancing the electromagnetic grid system of Earth to prevent major disasters, they've been given permission by the Godhead.

---

*I know you generally do this for individuals, but what would you say the dimensional vibration is of planet Earth today, if you could put a number on it?*

Planet Earth is midway through fourth density consciousness, a little over 4.5 in vibration. Humanity is at about 3.75 vibration, three-quarters of the way through third dimension. So, there's about a three-quarters gap in vibration between the composite vibration of humanity and the ambient vibration of Earth. And this is one of the reasons why some human immune systems are failing and why exotic viruses and bacteria are having a greater impact, because humanity has, as a whole—or at least three-fourths anyway—not been able to get out of third density consciousness, which is victim and conformity consciousness.

There's a popular word now going around some circles which is *sheeple*, meaning people who behave like sheep, blindly following a teacher or a guru or celebrity, causing them to be more and more out of phase with the vibration of Earth. Eventually, many of them will incarnate on other third density planets, because they're just not ready to be part of a fourth density Earth. The universe has scales and balances and infinite compassion for these souls, and there are many other star systems where they can stay longer in third density until they're ready to move on.

---

Sal Rachele, absolutely fascinating! I thank you and The Founders for your transmission, for your support, and for the love that's evident. Do you have any parting words?

We just want to say that we love each one of you and that we have most enjoyed this time.

---

*To find out more about Sal, his books, and The Founders, please visit Sal's website at www.salrachele.com.*

# Chapter 3

## Living as an Ascended Master on Earth *with Sara Landon*

### About Sara

Passionate about living her highest potential, Sara Landon is a guide for leaders, way showers, and changemakers contributing to raising the vibration of the planet. She shines a light on the path for others to expand beyond the perceived limitations of the human experience and live as the masters that they are while remaining grounded in the modern world.

As channel of The Council, Sara strives to be the ultimate student of the wisdom and teachings she receives. She is committed to mastering conscious, impeccable creation. Her intention is to be the purest channel of a grander perspective of what is possible and to help others discover that they have the same ability to connect to higher levels of consciousness and guidance.

Sara holds the vision of living in a fully awakened world where all beings live harmoniously with one another, the planet, the animals, and within themselves. She helps those who are ready to play in new levels of energy reconnect with all that they are so they may live, love, and lead in this time of awakening.

She is the author of three recent best-selling books, *The Wisdom of the Council* and *The Dream, The Journey, Eternity, and God* (co-written with Mike Dooley), and *You Are A Channel.* In each, she and The

Council share that those who summoned their words are here, now, to come into the realization of their true spiritual nature and to begin living as the master they truly are.

---

*Greetings, dear Council! Shall we begin?*

---

We are so pleased and delighted to have the opportunity to speak with you. And we remind you that, while our words to you are important, this is a vibrational experience of remembering the truth of who you really are, why you are here, and all that you intended when you chose this magnificent life experience. Because we assure you, your life is meant to be so very good for you.

## Living as an Ascended Master on Earth

The purpose for your life is joy and freedom. The reason you chose to incarnate on this magnificent planet at this time is to be part of the greatest awakening—the greatest transformation of human consciousness that has ever occurred in any lifetime. It is the raising of your vibration and consciousness, your own awakening, and your own great transformation that is positively contributing to the great transformation of human consciousness.

You chose to be here during this magnificent moment where humanity would remember the truth of who they are. As humanity fully awakens—as you remember—you are contributing to the possibilities, potentials, and opportunities for all humankind. Indeed, humanity and your beloved Mother Earth have a far greater purpose in this vast and glorious universe.

We tell you that the most important thing for your life experience is to fully come into the realization of all that you are. Realization is the integration of every part of you into the power that is you, into the love that is you, and into the force field of consciousness that is you.

You are magnificent, and you are opening fully into knowing that you are an ascended master here on Earth as you come into realization and embody the master that you are. All-That-Is asked you to stay on the planet as the embodied master that you are in your new levels of consciousness, vibration, and frequency: joy, love, freedom, abundance, well-being, and beauty. To live your life fully, whatever that means for you. To love fully, being all that you are in every present moment of your life.

You do this by not doubting or denying your worthiness or magnificence for any reason. Not because you didn't get this done or that done. Not because you feel a little bit frustrated or feel some resistance or got triggered. There is no reason ever to deny your worthiness or your magnificence or your power because you, dear master, matter. Your life matters, your love matters, and who you are matters, now more than ever.

Embody the master that you are. When you are in doubt of yourself or you are denying that you are loved, worthy, and more than enough, you hold yourself in separation. This lowers your vibration, limiting your consciousness, and doesn't allow you to summon the Source Energy available to you in every moment for the manifestation of everything you need and more, before you even know you need it, ordained by a higher level of consciousness.

Your soul is always out ahead of you, orchestrating on your behalf that which is in your highest and best good—that which will surprise, delight, and satiate you beyond anything your human[5] could ever think to ask for.

We know your physical senses are tuned to look at what is and consider it the only reality that's going on. But we want you to elevate your awareness and to perceive that there is so much more to you than you have ever allowed yourself to explore and discover.

You are a force field of consciousness. That is what you are. You are light, you are love, and you are a soul, but you are also a force field of consciousness that is summoning energy into form. You are here for that very formula. To manifest the form of whatever you want more of—more abundance, more love, more joy, more freedom, more well-being, more creativity, more inspiration, more of everything—because that is what leads to your expansion and the expansion of consciousness, expanding the potentials, possibilities, and opportunities for all humankind.

You are here as an ascended master on Earth. If you are reading this now, you drew this to you. You have channeled this information

[5]The Council refers to your egoic and physical perspective as "your human."

to you. You have drawn to you the knowing of who you really are and why you are here. You are us and we are you, and we come forth because we promised we would, so that you would no longer forget who you really are. We come to remind you of the power that you have to create your reality and that, in every moment, you can tune in to the force field of consciousness that is you and summon the energy that creates worlds.

## Your Force Field of Consciousness

You are now creating your world and your reality.

Reality moves *through* you, and as you raise your consciousness and vibration your destiny comes to you. That which is in your highest good, that which is your highest purpose, that which is your highest potential, and that which is your highest joy will present itself to you, because you are no longer imposing an experience of separation on your reality.

Heaven on Earth, or a New Earth, is not out there somewhere after you ascend or make your transition from this place out of the body. It's not a place you go. It's a state of consciousness, and it's available to you in every moment, no matter what.

Imagine, if you will, Heaven on Earth and what that means. Think of the beauty, peace, joy, abundance, harmony, well-being, freedom, and love that would exist for all. This is what you're here to create, dear master: your Heaven—your New Earth reality. Because as you do, you'll create a pathway that makes it easier and easier for all of humankind to find their way back to the truth within themselves, too, and to come into the realization of all that they are.

You can rid the world of anything you want. Through raising one's consciousness, you can attain freedom, joy, peace, harmony, well-being, and abundance. Not through force, effort, fear, fighting, and separation, but by creating them within. Then, you will positively impact your entire human family, allowing all those who are ready to remember that they, too, can choose whatever they want for themselves.

Realization, which you may also call enlightenment, is available to you every moment. But you beloved humans—and we love you so much—are still trying to do, do, do more and more and more, yearning and striving to be good enough, to earn a living, to feel worthy of the things that bring you joy—to feel worthy of doing the things you love and to finally feel worthy of playing and having fun. But it simply doesn't work that way.

There's never a reason to deny your worthiness and your magnificence. There's nothing you can do here on this planet to justify your radiance, magnificence, and brilliance. You are more than enough. And the proof that you are more than enough is that you are here in physical form at this time. Let go of all the things you need to do, or think you should do, or are supposed to do, because as you've already found, there's always more to be done.

From a state of being in your power in the moment, from the state of being in self-realization, from the state of enlightenment or Heaven on Earth, all things are done through you. Again, reality moves through you. Your destiny comes to you. This is because the force field of consciousness that you are is made up of particles of Infinite Creation that are always responding to you.

Understand this: the particles of Infinite Creation are all around you. When you expand your consciousness, your force field expands causing more of those particles to respond. And you expand your consciousness by doing more of what brings you joy, doing what you love, and doing what you're excited about. Then, everything you need, and more, will come to you before you even know you need it.

You do not get what you want. No. *You get what you are.* You get more of what you're perceiving, more of what you're feeling, and more of what you're focused on. So when you focus on the abundance you have, there will be more. When you focus on the love that you have, there will be more. You will be drawing more of the same to you because those particles of Infinite Creation are always responding. It's through the raising of your consciousness and aligning it to the truth of who you are that you summon the energy to move manifestations and True Creation into your reality.

You have no greater purpose than to live your highest potential, your highest excitement, and your highest joy in every moment. That is the greatest thing you can do to contribute, serve, and positively impact humanity and your world.

*Pertaining to self-realization, where does intention come in? Is that even important?*

*Does possessing the intention to awaken negate it? Should I have the intention to awaken—or should I simply pursue joy through, for example, hanging out with my young daughter?*

*The idea of surrendering is a tricky one for somebody like me. How do we find the balance between "intention and deliberate awakening" versus "just go out and have a great time, be happy, and love will abound"?*

Well, a few things for you here that would be very helpful. Number one, anything you love has the ability to awaken you. *Anything* you love, including your daughter: being with her and the love that you feel for her. When you think about the day she was born and the love you felt or when you think about those moments that you've loved her the most, you were as close to realization and enlightenment as you could possibly be, entirely because of the way you felt. What did you feel? Love pouring through every cell of your body; the light of the world shining within your heart.

Now, what do you think enlightenment feels like? It is the presence of the Divine—Divine love. It is the presence of God. It is Source, right in front of you, within you, and all around you. In every cell of your body, you're feeling that. That's what self-realization is. That's what enlightenment is. That's what ascension is. So, any person you love, anything that someone loves—really, really, really loves and is passionate about, even science or mathematics—has the power to awaken them, expand their perspective, their awareness, and their ability to perceive beyond, and to feel into a state of realization or enlightenment. That is the quickest path. It could be no other way.

For the intention of self-realization, we're going to talk about being in the moment, being present, and imagination.

Imagination is the realm of pure potential, available through being present in the moment. It's the raising of one's consciousness to explore different potentials for True Creation and bringing about experiences, dreams, and desires through the process of impeccable creation.

When you imagine yourself living as an ascended master, enlightened and realized, you project a holographic image into your force field of consciousness that the particles of Infinite Creation will respond to. And as they do, just as for all manifestations, you will be presented with the highest manifestation in a form that aligns with the original feeling of your intention—all done in the most easy, effortless, harmonious way possible, through the *process* of True Creation.

Maybe imagine yourself walking out in the sunshine with the biggest smile on your face and a breeze in your hair, birds and butterflies and the beauty of nature all around you, with your daughter skipping and jumping beside you and your beloved wife. Feel abundant with well-being in your body, joyful, and in harmony with everything. *Really feel this.* Can you see this by yourself? Can you even expand this vision of what enlightenment would look and feel like, going even deeper? That's your part. That's your job. That's what you're there to do.

Then completely let go of how, when, or where it's going to happen. Free yourself from any expectations of what may happen next, because quite honestly, you've already created it. You just focused yourself through the power of your imagination to draw from the realms of possibility available to you in the now moment. You created it. You've physically moved yourself through your consciousness, summoning energy into an experience where you will feel the reality of being fully realized. This is living as the enlightened master that you are.

Let the next perfect step come to you. Do this by following the energy, letting the light guide your way, and doing what is your highest joy, your highest excitement, what lights you up, what you love.

Now, we know you have a business and a lot of responsibilities: things that you do for your family and things you do for your employees and community. We understand there are all these things on your plate. But you love this; you love what you do. You love and have so much joy in this. So, bring that love and joy into the tasks that you're doing, knowing that you are *choosing* to do them, not because you *have* to but because you *get* to. If, in any particular moment, a task is not lighting you up, does not feel in the flow, and does not feel very joyful, then stop.

People spend their lifetime doing what they should do, what

they're supposed to do, or all the things they have to do because they're feeling "not enough yet," "not worthy yet," or "can't go have fun yet." Instead, you can train yourselves very quickly and easily, if you stop trying to push and force energy where you think it should go.

Don't continue to follow that unconscious program. Just stop in the moment and take some breaths. Catch yourself when you're trying to push and force energy where you think it should go. All your power lies in any now moment. Once there, let inspiration guide; it knows what's lighting up for you. Inspiration knows where the energy is. Inspiration comes from your soul, your Higher Self, your team, your guides, or whatever you want to call it. It's coming from the higher mind—from a higher level of consciousness and awareness beyond the limitations of your physical senses.

Inspiration is an impulse. It says, "I should do this, but I'm not going to push and force energy." "I'm going to stop and take some deep breaths." It asks, "What would bring me joy?" "What would really feel fun?" "What am I inspired to do in this moment?"

It might be something seemingly unrelated to your intention: Maybe the desire to visit a local coffee or sandwich shop or go get a meal for yourself. It could be to go for a walk or a run. These things don't seem related at all to what your intention was, but that's what's lighting up, so you go. A sign shows up. Synchronicity presents itself. You overhear a conversation, and all of a sudden, the next perfect inspiration comes to you, perhaps this time around the original intention.

This is following energy and letting light guide the way. It doesn't mean you don't take action. In fact, you take a lot of action, but it becomes inspired action. It's not action like you used to take from force and effort stemming from lack, limitation, separation, fear, or resistance. It's action that comes through inspiration, which is really what you want more of. More inspiration, more creativity, more enthusiasm, more passion, more divine orchestration, more synchronicities, more magic, more miracles, and more of all those things that are really natural when you raise your vibration and consciousness to live as the ascended master you are.

Anyone and everyone can do this. You all have this ability. You all have this power. You are all worthy of living a life that you love, doing the things that bring you joy. You're worthy of the freedom to be who you are, to live fully, and to love fully. You're worthy of abundance. You're worthy of well-being. You're worthy of love.

You're worthy of True Creation showing up even before you know you need it. You're worthy of that, which is why we say self-worth is the foundation of realization and enlightenment. If you still think there's something you need to do in order to be good enough to be an ascended, enlightened, or realized master, you'll never get there because there's nothing you *can* do to earn what's already the truth of you. Does that make sense?

---

*It does make sense. But we also hear about doing "the inner work," an implication that we're not worthy or at least not ready.*

You will not hear that from us.

---

*No, we did not hear that from you. But might we have some baggage or unfaced issues, unresolved fears, or unacknowledged grievances that need to be aired out?*

In the moment of realization, the past is healed. Everything is whole. Realization is to come into your wholeness, your perfection, your completeness, your magnificence. It's the integration of every part of you in the wholeness that is the truth of what you are.

Let us quickly cover levels of consciousness.

## Levels of Consciousness

### *The Third Dimension*

You are the mass conscious collective. Humanity, that you are part of, is most often in a state of the third dimension, which is determined by one's level of consciousness and one's vibration or frequency. When you're overwhelmed, frustrated, in resistance, busy, pushing, triggered—all those things—you're lowering your vibration. When you're telling yourself a story about why you can't do what you want to do, why you're not good enough yet, all these people who harmed you, and all these things you did wrong that you should be ashamed of, you're going to considerably lower your vibration and move into an experience of separation.

In separation, there is lack. You are separate from what you want. There's limitation. There's fear. So then you go out to push and force and effort in your lower vibration. There is no judgment from our side, ever; however, all the things you wish to rid the world of are happening in a lower level of consciousness. This is why raising your consciousness level out of separation, lack, limitation, fear, and suffering is the only path forward for those who want to live in a New Earth, Heaven on Earth, or in an ascended, enlightened, or realized state of consciousness.

You are not going to rid the world of all the bad things from a lower level of consciousness. It is through raising your own and elevating yourself that you'll create a pathway forward for all humankind, once they're ready to choose this for themselves.

When you begin to ask the question, "Who am I?" and you begin to understand you're not your circumstances, you're not your conditions, you're not your stories, you're not the unhealed parts of you, and you're not the things that keep you in limitation, you'll begin to realize you can change your stories and all else—which our audiences already know or they wouldn't have found this information.

### *The Fourth and Fifth Dimensions*

As you elevate your consciousness through the raising of your vibration into what we call the fourth dimension, you enter into a dimension based on transformation. In this dimension, you can change and transform. You can change your body, circumstances, and conditions. You can heal your body or heal past trauma. You can do the work to change things and fix things. You can determine what you want and manifest it. It's a dimension of transformation. Many remain here for years, decades, and sometimes, a lifetime, constantly trying to transform, change, and judge what they don't like.

Still, everything on your journey serves you.

The final step out of the fourth dimension into the fifth dimension is to let go of judgment of yourself, your body, and others. Anytime you're in judgment, you're going to entangle yourself with needing to further fix, change, or heal in order to feel worthy or deserving of whatever you want.

The fifth dimension is of pure love, where your well-being and abundance are assured. Every part of you is integrated into a state of oneness and enlightenment. You know the master that you are.

---

*Wouldn't moving with joy, instead of viewing it as "doing the work," actually force any unreconciled patterns, denials, or judgment to come bubbling up? Then, of course, we'd see them, integrate them, and continue on our merry way?*

Some might call the seeing and integrating "work." Either way, you've certainly painted a clear picture of how we can overdo self-analysis.

It is your soul's desire for you to experience, expand, and create in the fifth dimension. So, instead of using the word *work*, we would use the word *awareness*. Are you going to continually have new levels of awareness? Are you going to expand your awareness? Absolutely. Are you going to have a level of awareness around things that you never were able to perceive before? Are you going to be able to perceive beyond? Are you going to have a new and grander perspective? Yes. That doesn't need to be work. That's an exciting, beautiful, amazing, magical, extraordinary journey—or adventure, as Mike likes to call it.

There will always be new levels of awareness. There will always be new ways to perceive. There is always a grander perspective. We hold the vibration of that being an adventure versus working on yourself, processing, and clearing. There's no judgment from our side, but when you know how worthy you are, realizing all that you are, there'll just be more awareness, more to perceive, grander perspectives about all this, and more opportunities to live fully, love fully, and to be all that you are.

*You were speaking of third, fourth, and fifth dimensions. Where are we and what's going on right now? Would it be fair to say we're in fourth dimension right now, just having emerged from the third?*

It's not as fixed as you're describing it. You might have a moment of being in third dimension, and you catch yourself trying to push and force energy out of fear or separation. When you catch yourself, take a couple of breaths, and then focus on what brings you joy, what you love, and what excites you. Then you feel inspiration, you follow the energy, and suddenly, you're experiencing a moment of pure love with a bird or a butterfly or a tree that looks more beautiful than you've ever noticed before. Maybe you go out into nature, in a state of allowing, still doing what brings you joy, and these incredible synchronicities or miraculous moments present themselves. Now, you're in the fifth dimension.

Then you go home, your spouse is upset about something, and you're trying to fix it to make it better for them, and in doing so, you've slowed your vibration and lowered your consciousness a bit. Maybe now you're in the fourth dimension.

It's always determined by your level of consciousness, which is determined by your rate of vibration or your frequency. When that becomes the most important thing to you—the level of consciousness you're in and the level of vibration and frequency you're in—then you'll understand how to master living in higher levels of consciousness no matter what is going on in the world around you.

*The world is clearly in transformation. Is this about the Age of Aquarius? The Mayan calendar ending and a new one beginning? The Book of Revelation? It's a bit unsettling, but I believe there are also reasons to be excited. Still, why now? What's going on?*

We understand all these names and labels you give things. But when you label anything, you begin to limit the magnificence of creation. You are pure potential, and anything and everything is possible for you; you are creating your reality.

Now, when you come across something like the Age of Aquarius—and we're not disagreeing with that at all—something that says, "This is an incredible time in history where the vibration is higher, the consciousness is higher, and people are going to be stepping into their light bodies," it resonates with you as truth. "Oh, yes, it's the Age of Aquarius, because I'm reading all this stuff and it confirms all I know." But you don't have to wait for anything to happen to create it within your reality right now.

What's going on in the world around you is purely determined by your perspective. There are some that would say there's now more abundance on your planet than ever before, you have a higher level of consciousness than ever before, you are living in higher vibrations, and there's more love and more conscious people than ever before. If these are your perspectives, then these are the realities you'll experience.

If you're in a perspective where the whole world is at war, the planet is being destroyed, "It's wrong and bad, they shouldn't do those things, and now there's so much suffering"—this is determined by the level of consciousness you're in, preventing you from seeing a higher perspective of what's really going on.

Now, we understand, especially for our audiences, that you have this incredible love for the planet, animals, and humanity. You want to make this world a better place. You want to make an impact and a difference, which is why you're here. But you've known all along that you couldn't get into a low level of consciousness, into fear, separation, and judgment, to fight all the injustice thinking that was going to change things. In fact, that seems so silly to your soul or your Higher Self or that deeper knowing within you.

One of you in that fifth dimension of pure love has the power to expand your force field and hold such a powerful presence that others who walked into your field of consciousness would experience love, peace, joy, and harmony. They may even spontaneously awaken, coming into an absolute knowing of who they are just by being in your presence when you're in a realized state of pure love. That's the power you have.

Now, we're not saying you shouldn't take action on the things that you're passionate about. What we're saying is that you'll be wildly more effective at creating the changes you wish to see when you first get into a higher level of consciousness, raise your own vibration, and then take action from a grander perspective, unentangled with the lower energy of others.

---

*So, it's not important what's going on with the planet. What's important is what's going on within ourselves?*

---

When you begin passing judgment on the behavior of others, you are entangled. And from there, you begin drawing circumstances into your reality from the experience of separation. But the behavior of others really wasn't in your reality to begin with.

---

*"When so-called bad or negative things happen in my life, how should I think about those things? Does that mean I've been attracting the wrong things?"*

---

There is no bad or negative in that way. Over time, you'll see how every experience can make you more loving and compassionate. Whatever happened may have helped you remember your power or helped you get clear on what you really wanted. Looking back, you can see that what happened was really happening *for* you, and it was just your judgment, from an experience of separation, that made it appear bad or awful.

If you're judging something as bad or wrong, you're in an experience of separation, because that's the only place that bad or wrong exists. From our perspective, there is nothing bad or wrong. There are things that are happening in different levels of consciousness, but all is of love, Source, God, or the Divine.

In any moment, in every situation, there's always a grander perspective. If you allow yourself to move into that level of awareness, now and forever more, it will instantly manifest a sense of peace and knowing in your every moment.

When one forgets who they are and is in a lower level of consciousness, lowering their vibration such that they're experiencing incredible resistance, fear, or separation, and those feelings cause them to go out and take action that you would deem as wrong or bad, we see the truth of who they really are, and we know that these things are happening because of their level of consciousness.

We do not talk about the different levels of consciousness to impose any level of judgment or hierarchy. You came here to explore different levels of consciousness. You have been all things. Even in the experience of separation, you're still expanding who you are.

Every single moment and every single situation is an opportunity, a potential, and a possibility presenting itself to you. What you are expressing gives meaning to everything and determines your reality. If you focus on this thing that's really bad and the meaning you give it is really bad, that will be your reality, and you'll naturally be in resistance and fear of it. Take the exact same thing and focus on it from a higher perspective—choose to see it as an opportunity, potential, or possibility—and that will become your reality.

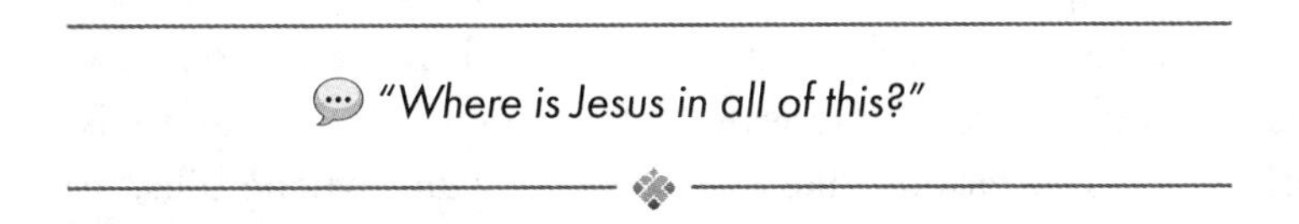


The being you refer to as Jesus, who is also referred to as the Christ (the awakened one), was of a consciousness and vibration of pure love, which, right here, right now, is also available to you. His teachings of love—love thyself, thy God, thy neighbor with all your heart—recognized that all of these are thyself. Because from the highest levels of consciousness, there is no separation. There is only right here, right now, in pure love. That is the truth of you. This is where Jesus is.

## Creating from Innocence

---

💬 *"You have spoken about the state of innocence while creating. Can you describe more about what that state is like, why it's important, and how it helps us manifest more quickly?"*

Think about an innocent child or yourself as an innocent child—a twinkle in your eye, playing on a warm summer day out in the grass, the sunshine on your face, maybe twirling around or running into the house to put a towel over your shoulders so now you're Superman or Superwoman or a king or a queen or whatever inspired your imagination.

A child in their innocence allows themself to experience those kinds of realities, not seeing any limitation or lack in being able to do so. They're going for the feeling. Then, suddenly, they decide it would be really fun to swing on the swing set. They revel in their freedom. When they feel hungry, they run inside to get a snack, after which they might paint a picture. And this continues, all day, until they go to sleep, ready to repeat the same tomorrow.

They don't worry that they need to make more money. They don't paint a picture and try to sell it for a thousand dollars, motivated by a sense of lack, limitation, or fear about paying bills. Yet, at some point, this is what happened to you. You all moved out of your innocence into worrying about what you should do, what you're supposed to do, and what you have to do. You want approval. You want to please others. You want to earn. You want to be enough. Your creativity is now driven by expectations, like making money and paying bills, fearing the consequences if you don't.

When you come back into the alignment of innocence, you can allow True Creation to be inspired in the moment. You can create from joy, love, and passion. And you'll actually be a far more powerful creator, creating for the joy of creating. Playing for the fun of playing. And in that, you will summon even more energy and have more manifestations, experiencing even more True Creation. When you're lowering your consciousness into separation or lack or limitation, you're limiting the amount of energy that you can summon into form.

In your innocence, you already know you're more than enough. You're free.

## Sleep, Pain, and Alzheimer's

*"What does our consciousness do while our body sleeps? Is it different for everyone?"*

Your consciousness does not reside merely in your brain or body. You are a force field of consciousness that is far more than what you know yourself to be. Even when someone makes their transition, their consciousness doesn't leave and go elsewhere. It's still here. Consciousness doesn't go anywhere; you're always one with Source.

However, when you're in an experience of physical form, creating reality, there's a part of you that is focused in and through your physical body, while simultaneously, there's a far greater part of you, call it your soul or your spirit or your Higher Self, that is not in an experience of time and space, that is ever-present and eternal and always one with All-That-Is.

*"How can I work with chronic physical pain and limitation as an ascended master?"*

First off, do not deny your infinite well-being, your health, your vitality, or your energy for any reason. We understand that when you have physical pain in the body, it gets a lot of your attention. But the more you can come into the moment and, therefore, your power—getting out of the story, the diagnosis, etc., and really come into the moment and feel into the ascended master that you are—the more your vision and experience will be drawn to your natural inclination of health and recovery.

The process for creating more of anything that you desire begins by simply going into your heart and really feeling what it will be like to have it. In your case, feel and imagine freedom, mobility, ease, and joy. It doesn't matter what else is going on—a disease, diagnosis, or pain. For just a moment, go into your heart, come into your power, and really feel what you want to feel.

What else do you want more of? Maybe more freedom? Go into your heart and feel it. Direct every cell of your body to align with the vibration of freedom. Feel it all the way up to the top of your head and down to the bottom of your feet. Allow yourself to feel into the infinite well-being that exists in this moment and is always available to you, raising your consciousness, raising your awareness, and raising your vibration to feel the desired alignment. Then breathe into this moment because it feels so good.

You can do this in any moment with anything. In such moments, you are literally expanding the force field of consciousness that is you, and the particles of Infinite Creation, which are in every cell of your body, will begin aligning themselves (or in some cases have already completely aligned) to the freedom, health or whatever it is.

Your cells are regenerating and rejuvenating based on your level of vibration and frequency. The more you're in a higher vibration and a higher frequency, feeling joyful and peaceful, the faster your cells are regenerating and rejuvenating themselves to align with the frequency that you are evoking in that moment. You are creating that reality of infinite well-being. If you stay in the feeling of that, you will experience in your reality that infinite well-being.

---

*"I have two elderly parents with Alzheimer's. They're often unhappy and anxious. How can we help our loved ones with Alzheimer's, and what is Alzheimer's from?"*

At this time on Earth, you have more diseases on your planet because this is where your focus has been. We could talk about each one, but essentially, they all arise when you entangle with certain beliefs or frequencies.

As humanity elevates its consciousness and remembers the truth of who you are, any misalignment of beliefs and frequencies become so obvious, you will immediately begin realigning yourselves back into peace, joy, love, and harmony. Then, within one generation, you will eradicate every disease on your planet. It all happens through the raising of consciousness and vibration.

You're on a journey of expansion through new levels of consciousness and vibration, where you're embracing a much higher perspective than the old ones of "oh, this is so terrible," or, "it's just the way it is," or "everybody in my family has it" to where, even today, there's a new understanding that every disease may be something emotional that's manifested in the physical body.

If your emotions are joy, peace, harmony, and well-being, then that would be the manifestation in your body. Whereas, anytime you're fighting something "out there," when you're worried about someone, when you're stressed out, pushing against a political party, fighting against something, or you're arguing in your head about why someone's wrong, all that energy moves through you first. You may be thinking negative thoughts about someone else, but your body doesn't know that. Your energy is moving through you. You may think you're fighting some agenda or person out there, but your body doesn't know that. Your cells in your body are "who" is really experiencing it, and so they begin to fight themselves.

So, what can you do when it's your loved ones? Love them. Whether they have a mental illness, Alzheimer's, or cancer, or they're struggling with money or a relationship, just love them. Just love them. See them as the truth of who they are because they, too, are a master; they, too, are a divine being. In that moment, they may not remember their power. They may not know the love that they are. But when you remember and know, when you hold your perspective and awareness on the truth of who they are, you will be bringing that state, or that frequency, of pure love into the moment. You may notice they start feeling better and better in your presence. Not because you're doing anything to them, but because by raising your vibration and frequency, staying in a state of pure love, you will help them to feel or align so much easier, through vibrational resonance, with that pure love.

One who has Alzheimer's is spending a lot of time in other levels of consciousness. Then they have moments of focusing back into this very dense, heavy consciousness, and so there's resistance. Just love them. Don't see this as anything wrong. We understand you want your loved one to be the way they were; you want them to be happy or normal again. What they're experiencing most of the time is themselves as the pure love, vibration, frequency, and consciousness that they are. If you begin to tune your awareness and your perspective on that, you'll start to see it more and more.

---

*Beautiful. Thank you so much, Council. My biggest takeaway is that we're good to go. We're ready, cleared for takeoff, and yet, we're already there.*

We say this time and time again. It's the basis of everything. We're here to help you remember you are everything you wish to be. You already are. It's all within you and it always will be. Anything and everything is possible for you through the process of raising your consciousness and summoning energy that will move into the form of grand manifestations with more magic and miracles in your life.

Get into the feeling. Imagine the highest vision you can for yourself. Imagine your highest excitement, your highest joy, and the grandest thing that you can imagine for yourself—the grandest reality that you wish to experience. Feel it and feel it and feel it and feel it, and then let it go. Do what brings you joy, and go do what you love. Follow the energy. Let the light guide the way. Let the next step come to you.

Reality is moving through you as this force field of consciousness that you are. In the raising of your consciousness, the energy can do anything. Your destiny will come to you. What you want and what you need will be there even before you know you need it, and you will live and create a life beyond your wildest dreams, we assure you.

We are always with you. We are always available to you. We love you, we love you, we love you. And with that, just for now, we are complete.

---

*To find out more about Sara, her books, and The Council, please visit Sara's website at www.saralandon.com.*

# Chapter 4

## The Role Love Plays in Self-Realization
*with Matt Kahn*

### About Matt

Matt is an incomparable spiritual teacher, highly attuned empathic healer, powerful speaker, and captivating author. He enriches people's lives by providing heart-centered solutions that ignite, delight, and unite. Matt wrote the highly acclaimed books *Whatever Arises, Love That; Everything Is Here to Help You* (featured in the "Be Kind" box by Ellen DeGeneres); and *The Universe Always Has a Plan*, which have been translated into more than a dozen languages.

His newest book, *All for Love: The Transformative Power of Holding Space*, won a Gold Independent Publisher Book Award and an Ommie Award (World Vision category) and is topping best-seller lists. Matt has become a YouTube sensation with his healing and often humorous videos. With more than 22 million YouTube channel views, followers are finding relief from the challenges of daily life through his messages of love. Among his honors, Matt was named one of the top 100 Most Spiritually Influential Living People by *Watkins Mind Body Spirit* magazine, alongside the Dalai Lama and Eckhart Tolle.

# Prelude

## Non-Trance Channeling

*Hi, Matt! We're honored to have you with us. Before we begin, can you explain a little bit about your method or style of channeling?*

So good to be with you again, Mike.

Going way back, when I was a kid, I'd say things that just kind of jumped out of me, and it would feel like someone else was talking through me. It wasn't until my late teens that my guides started speaking to me. The first thing they said was: "You're not who you think you are." My response was, "Who the hell are you?"

I've continued to have these very matter-of-fact conversations with guides, archangels, and ascended masters on my very progressive path of awakening. These became both my initiation into being a channel and my indoctrination for the journey I'd be taking people on.

It was a surprising turn of events. Suddenly, I was this spiritual guy talking to ascended masters. I asked them every question I could think of, sometimes repeating the same question just to see if their answers would change. Not only did they remain consistent, but everything always felt loving, safe, and all about unity consciousness. For a long time, I remained skeptical. I wanted to connect with my guides, but there was a part of me that was afraid I was making it up—I didn't want to force or fake anything.

There eventually came a time when trust was established, and I was told that I would be transmitting healing energy. I said, "I don't want to step aside and let someone or 'something' else talk through me." They said, "Well then, you're going to have to go through a journey of integration and healing to be an embodied channel."

This excited me: the idea of creating a lifelong compendium of work on myself, serving as a model for what I was teaching, making myself the open space where this energy could flow, while being myself and becoming one with what I was accessing. Just having the Universe on speed dial would have been cool enough, but there was also a part of me that wanted my life to be a full commitment to my work.

I've developed an ability to transmit healing energy, foster awakening, and help people embody the kind of knowing that will make lasting changes. It's my deepest desire to help people awaken to their highest capacity and to know the true magic of the Universe that resides in us all.

I teach ideas I've never known before. I can literally go on stage, cold, and, like everyone in the audience, I'm hearing what's being said for the very first time.

I'm aware of the channeled words pouring through me. It's not something I come up with ahead of time and then share—which is fine, but that's not my process. I might know a little bit about what I'm going to teach, like today: awakening. Yet I'm not choosing the words; my words choose me.

The truth is, every one of us channels on some level. Most people, however, are only channeling their egos, instead of manifesting, embodying, and channeling their soul.

## The Ego, Higher Self, Spirit Guides, and Soul

*Do you ever have an egoic conversation with your guides? Does your ego talk to them, and then there's an exchange of ideas?*

There are moments when I realize my ego is getting agitated. Normally, I'm very clear in my decision-making. I always know exactly what I need or want to do in any given moment. In the odd moments when I waiver, thinking to myself, "maybe this…or maybe that," I realize my egoic operating system is being activated. I may honor it because the ego is necessary, to a degree. I just have to be careful, because it comes down to how transparent or dense its motivation is. The density of someone's ego is always reflecting the amount of psychic protection they think they need.

A lot of people express themselves through an embellished personality because, to them, it creates safety. It's when we're liberated beings, however, awakened in the oneness of truth, that we don't require as much protection. Then, our ego can shrink and be transparent, and we can become a vessel of individual expression for Source Energy.

I don't require a lot of protection, so it doesn't flare up that much. But when it does, I usually find it ruminating over some choice, until I laugh and move on with my day. Thankfully, with the channel and the connection to the Universe that I have, everything is very clear, very definitive, and very simple, and that's how I'm used to living my life.

---

*You don't feel the ego trying to claw its way back?*

No. In fact, I think that one of the reasons the ego does that is because we, as human beings, have to learn about our boundaries. A lot of people are still caught in a pattern of trying to be all things to all people. Trying to present the most likable, lovable version of themselves to others, which is great, but then we don't always act in a space of true authenticity.

For example, if you need space to recharge, but you're afraid to upset someone or think that they'll abandon you, then you're going to over-give. That's going to lead to depletion, exhaustion, and resentment. So, when the ego flares up, it's often acting on behalf of consciousness to either remind us of a boundary we don't know how to create or an imbalance that we're overlooking.

When we're living in a place of true autonomy and a place of true sovereignty, we're unconditionally loving and valuing our own time. Then we can share space with people without an over-giving that's going to deplete us or leave us feeling resentful.

This kind of lesson, along with many others, constitutes the evolution of our spirits in these human bodies—in other words, awakening.

---

*How do you begin to distinguish between the voice of ego versus Higher Self? How did you experience this evolution?*

I started to notice, within me and for a lot of other people, too, that when ego arises, there's often an element of time involved. For example, the ego uses cause and effect, superstition, manipulation, or ultimatums as a time-based device to create pressure. When it's your ego masquerading as intuition, it'll say you need to make this decision by this moment or else you're either going to miss out on something amazing or something catastrophically horrible is going to happen.

When we get into this kind of ultimatum-like conversation, it's actually our ego masquerading as our highest wisdom. The ego's not trying to hurt anyone; it's saying, "Look, you like to give your attention to spiritual things, so I'm going to dress up as your spiritual guide because I want some attention." It's like a kid saying, "Hey, Dad likes football—he watches it all the time—so I'm going to put on a football uniform and maybe Dad will give me more of his attention."

I've also found that when it's our ego at play, we tend to think we know more about other people than they know about themselves. When it's your soul, however, your awareness is about you and you alone. Other people are the mystery; you're the subject of self-awareness and self-responsibility. That's a big one.

---

*Do you feel it's your soul that comes through?*

I think of one's soul as a unique extension of the totality of Source. The way in which Source expresses itself through an individual. We could also say that the wisdom a soul accesses is your Higher Self. I use these terms interchangeably.

Then, I have spirit guides I work with, which is not unusual. If you look at the Hindu religion, for example, you'll find a variety of gods and goddesses who are simply unique expressions of the Divine. I find that our guides are simply individual attributes of our soul who offer wisdom from the Higher Self. This is also part of our awakening: bringing the wisdom of your Higher Self into your body to influence your language patterns and choices—to literally manifest spirit into your form.

### The Call to Awaken

The question is: How far will one go in their journey? How much are they willing to dedicate themself to the opportunity of allowing more truth into their life ? Maybe we've had successes in our lives, maybe disappointments, but to go farther, there comes a point where we say, "I'm less seduced by personal gain and less fixated with the fear of personal loss than I am ready to allow the Divine to work its most incredible magic through me, expressing its highest will for the benefit of this planet."

When we get to a place where we want to connect with something higher than gain and loss, and something more relevant and real than fear, superstition, and anticipation, it's because we're going through an awakening of consciousness that allows us to be vessels of spirit instead of just reflections of spirit's potential.

## Set an Intention

Now, as you're following this, I'd like you to set a private intention for this transmission, because I want you and your guides to be a part of this cocreation. We'll be collaborating on transmitting a healing energy that fosters your most profound awakening.

In honor of that, please take this moment to set your intention for what you hope to receive. For example, "I wish for it to help me: Heal. Awaken. Integrate. Embody. Feel safe. Be more connected to my own psychic messages and guides. Or all the above."

You don't have to pick one; you can name as many as you want.

Take a moment.

How will you direct this energy so that we can awaken and heal as one?

## The Role Love Plays in Self-Realization

### The Divine Feminine

Throughout history, every being that has ever awakened to a higher truth has satisfied an intention of the Universe, which was to create worlds where it incarnates as an individual, only to grow and experience the expansion of each along their journey, to satisfy its curiosity and know itself at the deepest levels. The more the Universe wakes up within each of us, the more the Universe expands as a whole, because reality is made from the fabric of an all-loving intelligence.

In the beginning of the journey, in what we would think of as the traditions of awakening and healing, we've been taught from a very masculine standpoint. Yet, because we've now reached a very pivotal time in history, often referred to as our ascension, the Universe wants to remember itself in a way it never has.

This ascension represents a returning of equal power for the masculine and feminine—an energetic balance within each human being. The more balanced, the more harmonious their external reality, ultimately raising the vibration of the planet, reversing the karmic wheel and global warming, creating a more sustainable world, and manifesting Heaven on Earth.

The divine feminine is all about love. The divine masculine is all about truth. True awakening is the marriage of both: when we love truth more than staying safe in fear-based avoidance and when the truth of love calls more greatly to our hearts than looking for things to fixate on or avoid.

I came into this journey not having studied the masculine teachings of awakening, but by actually experiencing the awakening of truth, the realization of a higher power that lives as you in oneness. What I noticed about the masculine aspects of awakening, in the absence of the feminine, is that it can sometimes make some truths seem more unreal or illusory, i.e., less relevant. This happens because it's the feminine that arouses the truth of love. The truth of love offers more of an expanded field of view.

Within the divine feminine, you know all is one and that, no matter how anybody behaves, we're all expressions of divinity. We're able to make personal decisions about our boundaries and no longer be accomplices to crimes committed against us. We're able to do this so skillfully with love as our guide, saying, "I can choose and hold space for my own sovereignty without disturbing or disrespecting the divinity in another," even when someone else's divinity may be so difficult to see due to their traumas and patterns at play.

When the divine feminine starts to arise within us, we start to realize love is a higher force; in fact, it's the highest vibration. You will embody it as your own highest vibration depending upon how much time and how much of your life you give to it.

## The Divine Masculine

Typically, in our unconscious world, the masculine awakens well before the feminine. So, we often perceive love as a reward for good behavior and something to withhold as a way of punishing those that are acting from a lesser aspect of themselves. Many children have experienced love in a disciplinary fashion.

On a spiritual level, we don't necessarily love in exchange for experiences we prefer and like. We love as a way of saying, "I am so inspired by the amount of pain I sense in this person (which I don't necessarily have to feel) that I can acknowledge it as their influence to act from their least redeemable aspects of character. Whenever someone's acting from their ego, it's because they're hiding, in pain, and feel unsafe. I'm not going to withdraw my love as a way of trying to discipline them. I'm going to hear their cry for love and offer what they need to heal so that they will no longer be taken advantage of and can be liberated from their plight of pain."

When the divine feminine wakes up, love is what we offer to ourselves and to every human being. We learn the difference between "I love you as a soul" and "I cannot tolerate your (egoic) mistreatment of me and others." Love is a way to balance out the masculine drive for truth. Otherwise, the masculine is only driven to explore truth, wandering around looking for its long-lost love, the divine feminine.

## Uniting Our Divine Energies

In awakening, we're uniting the masculine and the feminine. It's very interesting to state it this way because, very commonly, in the early stages of awakening, people adopt "spiritual" egos. Spirituality becomes another mask along the way. People trying to stand for a higher truth get so attached to it, they misunderstand people who see things differently. They may hide behind keyboards and be so into some political or philosophical truth that they fail to treat others with kindness.

When we awaken to love, we can stand for a truth that does not lower the standard of our character. We can represent a truth that does not require us to disrespect the sovereignty of any human being. And even when we're disrespected by others, we don't have to tolerate mistreatment when we're existing in a state of love. Neither does it touch, harm, or hurt us when we are whole as the love that we are.

I share this with you as I'm channeling, but also, as a person, I can reflect on my life and how it changed when love woke up within me—when I realized the role love plays in healing and awakening, and how it is all part of the same journey. We have to *emotionally* nourish ourselves with all the things the past seemed to withhold from us. We need to give ourselves the love that we wish we had more of from our parents. Maybe we were loved by a parent who died unexpectedly, and so we felt like the love left with them and we're grieving. Or sometimes people may have said, "I love you," while they did very unloving things, leaving us to distrust love.

The question is: Can we start to become the open space, the receivers, for love to wake up? Can we begin giving ourselves everything we need that seemed to be withheld in the past? Because when we give each wound the love that it lacked or the love it didn't remember receiving or the love that was absent during a moment of trauma or mistreatment, we bring to that memory the wholeness and completion of all experiences, which gives that memory permission to dissolve at a cellular level, return to the light, and transmute.

## Transmuting Trauma

So we can either mentally process our wounds—maybe comparing how a relationship ending reflects on our mom and dad's relationship or psychoanalyze anything else until the end of time—which is the traditional path of the masculine, or we can embrace a more unified, new paradigm approach, choosing to emotionally process our trauma. Either way, we must emotionally process our wounds to find the relief we seek.

Mentally processing is, "This happened. This also happened. What's the relationship?" Emotional processing is acknowledging that whatever feeling I'm having is a part of a cellular memory trying to complete its journey and return home to the light. If I can allow the feeling to be felt, if I can accept that it's a part of my highest path and give it the love it doesn't remember receiving from the past—even if the love I give it doesn't change how I feel—I'm now helping a part of me reach a journey of completion. I'm helping another memory or cluster of emotions transmute back into light.

The entire awakening process is literally the embodiment of alchemy: transmuting trauma and returning it to light. Only love can do that.

Even as we sit here together, maybe with our hands over our hearts, whatever we're feeling is the way we're meant to feel right now. What love would tell you, as I'm telling you, is that there's no reason for sad to be anything other than sad. Instead, just be the love that holds the sadness until it's ready to let go. There's no reason to make fear anything other than being afraid. We're not here to transform fear into love. We're here to love the one who's afraid. When I wrote *Whatever Arises, Love That*, there were people who thought I was trying to say, "Oh, this person betrayed me; I'm supposed to love that." Not my point. "That" is referring to the invitation to feel and free that which was blocked or resisted.

So, it's not, "My partner betrayed me and I love that," or "I should love it to make sure it doesn't happen in the future," which is more superstition. Instead, I say, "If I can feel how traumatizing it is to be betrayed, don't I deserve more love, not less, right now? If I can acknowledge how much love I deserve, can I focus more on giving myself the love that I desire, not focus and fixate on what someone did to me?"

Which doesn't mean that, from time to time, if someone does something egregious, you refrain from acting. It may require legal intervention or bringing someone to justice for a crime they've committed. We can follow through on whatever process of justice is required to ensure that more people won't be harmed in the way you may have been hurt. But we don't have to do it with a grudge in our heart. We don't have to match someone's karmic patterning by building more karma within ourselves. Karma is not about doing the "wrong thing," but unintentionally building more walls within yourself during your journey.

We want walls to come down with every step we take, not have new ones go up. And what keeps the walls down, what keeps the heart bursting open, and what allows you to truly taste the gravity of your own immortality is how much of yourself you hand over to love: living a life of giving yourself to love. When we don't give ourselves to love, we live in endless negotiation with the Universe and our imagination, intending and believing that everything has to go a certain way, overlooking the fact that the Universe has a plan for us and that we are cocreators on this journey with very important roles.

Don't compete with the Universe; harmonize with it. The way you harmonize in oneness with the Universe is by joining it in adoring and loving yourself the way it always has and always will. The Universe is having a profound experience knowing itself as you. Your separation from it is only the distance between how you see yourself and how the Universe sees you. The Universe sees you as a magnificent creation. If you see yourself less than that, you'll feel separate from Source.

The question is: How do we bridge the gap and become one with the Universe? By learning to see ourselves from a higher level of worth and esteem. Well, how do we do that without pretending or being inauthentic? We love the parts of ourselves that can't yet see how they're simply reflections of our own unprocessed pain.

This is not where we hide in high vibration to outrun low vibration. This is not where we give spiritual interpretations of reward and punishment or think that the Universe works in any cause-and-effect way. This is where we unleash the magnificence of our own eternal light.

In order for you to know how brightly you're shining and transforming this world, you have to turn that light onto yourself and taste the gravity of your own radiance. It can be intimidating. It's very intimate, yet the ego has nothing to control in intimacy. The ego also faces the ironic predicament of developing subconscious fears for the things it desires. So, while the ego seeks to fulfill a desire, it's also building a fear over its arrival, like when people fixate on trying to find their soulmate and go on first dates filled with anxiety.

## Embodied Love

Love is what helps us balance everything out. Love is what grounds us. Love is what fosters expansion. Love is what allows us to attract experiences, receive them, and step fully into them without running toward something that we're going to run away from the moment it shows up. Love makes everything right. Love brings wholeness to the planet. And love is the very force that heals and awakens all human beings.

Again, how much of your life are you willing to hand over to love? How much of yourself will open to let love in? We answer these questions by getting to know love and by getting to know love as who we are, not love as a manipulative force that makes your experiences change or as a love that is only present when you're feeling elated versus defeated. It's a love that is the very support that holds you in your greatest moment of triumph or your deepest moment of heartbreak.

Love is the very breath you breathe. Love is the eternal support of Source Energy. The more we love ourselves, the more we're able to love others, the more we're able to see others from the most innocent perspective, and the more we call forward only the versions of other people that match the love we've given to ourselves.

Love happens to be our most intrinsic form of psychic protection. It's the very identity of your essential nature. There's no wound love can't heal, and there will never be an evolution of consciousness where love is not at the forefront as the central focus of spiritual expansion, like right now. We're currently living in a world that's going through a revelation of expanded consciousness, just beginning to glimpse and taste a remembrance of unity—a remembrance that love is for everyone.

Soon, we'll no longer live in a world where everyone is trying to hide love for themselves out of the fear of not having enough or of missing out on experiences we're always meant to have. Love is an act of service. Love is not just where we embrace people for the decompartmentalized experiences we wish to have with them. It's an honor we bestow on all that says, "I will receive you, I will honor you, and I will care for you in the name of love."

Soon, we'll be living in an interdependent reality of unity consciousness, no longer making decisions only for our own personal gain or to avoid any degree of personal loss. Instead, we'll be making decisions that are always good for the totality of life, including ourselves, living in a sustainable level of consciousness—a level of consciousness I call village consciousness.

We live in a world, but the world is truly a collection of villages that will begin to thrive when we individually live for the well-being of each other. This is something we've lost sight of. As we accelerate the expansion of consciousness, we help run out the clock of *un*consciousness, and we'll literally speed up the fabric of time by how often and authentically we love ourselves and each other. Because, in the connection of light that is the unity binding us as one, when I love myself, I help heal in the world, and when I help heal in the world, I transform myself. Even if you thought, "I'm not interested in helping the world heal," just by loving yourself, you would transform yourself, and therefore, you would transform the world.

*How do we know where to begin healing ourselves when we've unintentionally allowed our ego to trick and delude us for so long—for a lifetime? We usually don't know that the ego has played such a clever role in our lives, yet we can often sense something is not right. How do we navigate to that place of recognizing what we most need, so that we can feel complete?*

There's a couple of ways we can go through this. First, look to your body for any kind of heaviness, pressure, or pain. If there's any kind of disturbance, locate it. Ask, "Where in my body do I feel this?" Then ask that part of your body, which has its own consciousness, "What are the words you need to hear from me in order to help you heal and move this energy?"

We're not just trying to move the energy. We're appealing to the consciousness of the body that says, "Hey, I'm a part of you. I'm actually one of your guides." Our job is to notice the disturbance as an attention-seeking device from the most innocent levels and to hear the whimpers and cries and pleas that show up as physical pain, exhaustion, or depletion that are actually circulating trauma-loop memories from our limbic system. Just locate where that is in your body and ask this part that feels separate. Honor its own separate consciousness by offering, "What do you need from me in order to take your next step of healing?"

Sometimes just asking that question won't elicit an immediate answer because that part of you needing help says, "Oh my God, I just love when you engage with me like this!" What it really loves is being able to give an answer from its perspective instead of it being projected upon like a parent who says, "I know what my child needs." Okay, maybe you do. But you can also ask the child, "What do *you* need?" If there's no answer, we can be the adult. But to engage these parts with the respect and sovereignty for their own consciousness literally opens the wound up and says, "Now I know that you are my faithful liberator, and I'll let you into this healing instead of trying to hide from you."

There's a part of every fear, however, that's afraid of its own death! Our wounds are afraid that their healing will be their death. In actuality, healing transforms shapes into different forms. If, however, a part of you identifies with one "thing" and you know healing is going to make you different, for the wound that feels like a death. Our wounds are hiding from the light, afraid of death, and our journey is to help these wounds realize, "I am love. I am here to rescue you. I am taking you into the light. You are being reborn. You fear that this is death, but I'm going to hold your hand and be with you so that you know this is a rebirth and not an assassination plot." We can and do love these parts by talking to them and getting to know these parts of ourselves emotionally versus mentally.

The ego often believes it can sidestep emotional connections with over-rationalization, but what we're realizing in this world is that doesn't work. It only creates imbalanced human beings and an unsustainable planet.

---

*Would you say that mastery of self, on a path of awakening and enlightenment, is about bringing love to areas of your essence that have not received it so far?*

I would agree with that a hundred percent, and I'll tell you why. Having taught in many communities and to people of various paths, sometimes—and it's an energy thing—I can walk into a room of beings that are on a hot path to awakening. There are certain audiences for whom awakening is *the* thing.

What I can feel, energetically and empathically, is when their heart is opening to a love affair with service, that's when the awakening is pure. Other times, I notice that they only want to wake up because they just hate being the character they can't stop being in their life. Then, awakening becomes a form of self-denial.

Some people look at awakening as, "I'm going to trade up to a bigger truth and get the hell away from this person I hate being. Maybe they'll give me a new 'IP address' and better manifestations." But true awakening comes when we love ourselves. The Buddha under the

Bodhi tree said, "I will not move. Everything comes to me." That's a stance of love. When we are loving, we are cultivating presence. We are not moving toward things; we're letting things move toward us.

The very path of loving ourselves puts us in an alignment that allows awakening to be triggered. But for people on the path who *haven't* done the emotional work, if they suddenly have an expansion of consciousness because the truth dropped in and broke them open, it can send them into a dark night of the soul.

If emotional healing comes first, awakening will happen along the way. Then, once awakening happens, we don't have to go into this crazy Willy Wonka boat ride and revisit all the things that we either didn't see or overlooked. By loving ourselves before and through awakening, we love ourselves after awakening. Love is playing a role at every stage. That's what we should align with first.

## The Dimensions

*Can you speak to the third dimension and fourth dimension? What's going on in the world right now? Is this polarity? Is this the Book of Revelation come to life? Is this the new Mayan calendar? What and why?*

Yeah, we're now living through "The Book of Revelation: The Musical." This is a very pivotal part of history. But just to understand dimensionally, third dimension is the dimension the Earth has been in for a long time. It's a dimension of individual expression. That's a positive thing. It's the dimension of determination, where you're willing to take a journey of time and allow things to evolve in what seems to be slow-motion compared to the instantaneous manifestation of quantum reality. Also, in third dimension, we're experiencing an individuality that makes us feel separate from one another, separate from each other's hearts, and separate from the Universe. The negative aspect of this dimension arises when we resist moving through it. We're not meant to stay here.

The fourth dimension is the dimension of time: the time we all require to embrace our individuality, to heal the wounds of the individual journey, and to allow the individual to be a unique expression of spirit. Fourth dimension is also where people get into spiritual teachings that are akin to fear-based superstition. It's really hot on conspiracy theories. It's like the Burning Man Festival of spiritual evolution.

Fifth dimension is unity consciousness, where, even though we're individuals, we also have the realization we are one. We're not so "one" that we lose ourselves, nor are we so into our individual consciousness that we overlook our oneness. It's a dimension of balance. It's the dimension where the internal expansion of your light starts to manifest outside of you and reflects back.

The third dimension is often the starting point where we are meeting ourselves as individuals. Then, we get to experience the expansion of the individual through a journey of time to realize the oneness that includes all things and that celebrates its oneness through a play of diversity. And from that space, as we start to really acknowledge diversity, we start to live in a different world, where all rules and ways of behaving encompass tolerance, inclusivity, and equality. So, right now, we're watching the incredible process of a world waking up, where society is transforming itself into a living expression of unity consciousness.

---

*Would you say that we are fourth dimension ever since 2012?*

The year 2012 was when Earth went four dimensional, and 2019 is when it went full five dimensional. And now, every one of us, if we're meant to continue, has to be a closer match to where Earth is. It's believed by many that until this happens, Earth can't further ascend. This is the reason why all hell is breaking loose; Earth has ascended into the fifth dimension and human beings must catch up.

---

*What might be some of the things we see or experience while this happens?*

We'll start seeing people, driven by their pain and wounds, beginning to take more responsibility for their behavior, instead of projecting these onto others and hiding in righteousness.

People will stop abusing one another once they become conscious of truth. The telltale sign of any villainous character is that they're convinced they're the hero. That's part of their delusion. What determines a hero from a villain is a hero always acts in a place of integrity for all. A villain uses integrity only with self-interest.

To get a little "Joseph Campbell," what we're going to start seeing in the hero's redemption is their unconsciousness becoming more self-aware and self-reflective. They'll even be able to communicate after the fact, "Hey, that wasn't my highest truth. I think I hurt you. I'm so sorry."

This is an evolutionary leap. And at the same time, there will be our own incredible superpowers and abilities that we start seeing made manifest. It's just a matter of which of these powers is most practical for the world we live in. The truth is, all of us are *already* experiencing other-worldly phenomenon.

## Dying in Order to Live

We're all evolving spiritual masters finally becoming aware of our mastery. As we each step into our mastery, we'll start to experience the space between things. We'll start to experience dimensions within dimensions. We'll start to experience waking life as a bigger dream state. Things just won't seem as real as they used to. We'll begin to "know" things on a level without needing the ego to confirm its validity. We'll finally be able to trust our feelings and allow the senses of our inner guidance to lead us as it becomes safer to face our feelings in the most loving way, where we start to live our lives fully present, from a place of humility not from a place of judgment.

For us to taste our timeless nature, we have to confront our own egoic mortality. I think one of the most amazing things about awakening is that it helps us endure and survive endless psychological deaths. Only by dancing with death in this way can love become the highest priority. Our old selves have to die in order to know how to live. Until we've experienced this, we won't know how to embrace the choice to love without it being an option that benefits the ego. The beauty of love as a choiceless choice is the greatest gift that awakening gives us.

When we awaken, we don't need to leave the body in order to transcend the limitations of our human condition. We can expand our consciousness to where it would be in the heavenly realm while staying within this Earth plane, still embodied, where that expanded energy can tangibly take shape and form as the Universe knowing itself at a more profound level than ever before.

## More on the Ego and the Games It Plays

---

*I want to quote your book* All for Love: *"...even if the ego constantly got its way, it would be no happier than before."*

*So, not only does the ego not know what it really wants, but when it gets what it thought it wanted, it's still not going to be happy! I think we can all relate to this. Can you tell us, what is ego?*

Ego is a spectrum of psychological density. It helps us be rooted and grounded on Earth. For example, if you had no ego, you would walk out into a snowstorm naked, forgetting to put on a jacket or clothes. Without ego, there's no sense of distinction, and you lose the ability to function in the world.

The ego helps us have the experience of being individuals in a world of other people. However, when ego is where you find your sense of identity, you wind up making decisions from the pain and patterning of unprocessed trauma instead of responding from the empowerment of your highest wisdom. When we identify with ego, it's common to believe, "I'm better than this person," or "That person's better than me." The ego likes to put itself, or other people, on a pedestal.

Then, of course, when we put people on pedestals, there soon follows a compulsion to tear them down, because we resent them for being bigger than we perceive ourselves to be. The ego inevitably unravels all it creates. It's quite a self-fulfilling prophecy.

And yet, from a higher perspective, all of this can be seen as the ebbing and flowing of a psychological density that helps loosen our grip of attachment and soften our edges for deeper healing to occur. Seeing this is not a judgment. It's just where one is in their journey, just as a butterfly would never judge itself for having the cocoon it needs in order to break free and be reborn. The question still remains, no matter where anyone is in their journey, "Can I love myself enough to face my patterns, instead of hiding my pain by comparing myself to others?"

---

*Are our egos a function of beliefs? Doesn't everything boil down to focus, thoughts, and beliefs? Can we work on these to lighten the load of our egos? Or do we simply need to shine more love on the ego?*

If we find limiting beliefs within ourselves, those beliefs are here to be loved. So, we say to the belief, "You are a part of me that's here to be loved." Typically, people want to watch their thoughts, track their beliefs, and unravel them as they deem necessary. This is a very masculine way of working with the masculine mechanism of mind. If we're going to understand the law of polarity, what the masculine mechanism needs is to be balanced by its opposite, a feminine vibration. In awakening, we're actually bringing the heart and mind into an equal space. The mind enters the heart. The heart enters the mind. If we find limiting beliefs, the limiting beliefs are healed as they are loved.

Limiting beliefs and thoughts are always reflective of the traumas we carry. The density of ego tells us how much work we've done or how much work needs to be done. All of which can only be resolved with love; otherwise, we're wrestling with ourselves on the battlefield of psychoanalysis. As consciousness awakens, we're not solving the mind's issue on the level of mind. We're letting the heart heal the mind, or letting the mind hold space for the heart, as they meet in the center of our being.

*But does the ego go away forever? Does it perish?*

The ego experiences its own death, but what it perceives as its own death is actually a rebirth of the soul. Because nothing in life really dies; it just changes shape and form. Just like when people die and leave the planet, they're going to a different dimension by changing shape and form. So, we may call it ego death, but it's the ego's rebirth.

The ego will never know rebirth until it's on the other side. Once it's on the other side, it's no longer as it was. The ego perceives change, or anything other than what it prefers, as death, which it seeks to avoid at all costs. So, what we are doing is being the love that's helping it adjust to its rebirth in spite of its fears.

*"When unpleasant things happen in our lives, is it because we've been attracting the wrong things or because we're not using the Law of Attraction properly?"*

Subjectively, we perceive things as positive or negative in our own way. Any judgment of "bad things" depends on our chosen perceptions. We alone decide what's positive or negative, and whatever we choose simply reflects our beliefs, not reality.

It's not like things or manifestations don't exist until we say so, and it's not like we're attracting havoc because our Law of Attraction muscles are broken. The Law of Attraction is more about being in alignment with spirit, and the things that we say we're going to create are the Universe's way of saying a manifestation is closer to you than you are to it. So, be still, open up, and allow it to be received in whatever form it wants to take.

That's a more detached view of how the Law of Attraction can actually free us from the grip of the ego's control instead of trying to teach us spiritual ways to control reality.

*"How do you make space for grief while also embracing our eternal connection to whatever was 'lost'?"*

Always make space for grief. The minute grief comes up, allow it to be felt and embrace it as the love of divinity holding all wounds as they heal.

Whenever we're consoling ourselves, we are on the same side as the Universe. We are divinity in form. In truth, there's no space between grief and eternal connection. It's just that paralyzing levels of grief seem so contrary to feelings of joy, connection, and expansion. Obviously, they're very different emotional states. But spirit is not any emotional state. Spirit is the infinite source of love that holds all emotional states, like waves coming and going in the ocean of existence.

Grief is a wave. Spirit is the ocean. Our breath is the remembrance that we are the ocean witnessing each wave. When we are consoling our feelings, when we're holding an emotional wave with love, we are then being the ocean, healing its waves, and helping create calmer waters versus choppier tides. This is the remembrance of spirit.

No matter how big a tidal wave becomes, it cannot threaten or drown the ocean holding it. No matter how painful our emotions may be or fearful any thought may appear, they're waves of expression requesting love return them home to the ocean from their adventure of seeking the shore. As we learn to love ourselves more, not less, we activate the power of divine remembrance that equally brings our healing journey to a place of resolution, while learning to shine our light at a higher frequency for the evolution of our world. No matter how conflicted or at the brink of extinction humanity may seem, in a world of endless questions, love is the only answer.

*"I'm taking care of an adult child with disabilities. Because of this responsibility, I can't pursue what I want in my life or even just be me. I'm getting older and tired. How can I feel better about this situation?"*

Whenever you're in the presence of someone with a disability or taking care of them—or for anyone experiencing a responsibility that seems to distract from what you wish to be doing with your life, which is heartbreaking to process and shame inducing—silently say in your mind, "Thank you for helping me. Thank you for helping me dedicate myself to loving service. Thank you for helping me remember that love is a choice, not a sacrifice."

If we are a caretaker of an adult child with disabilities, even as we feel the obligation of that choice, we have to find the space to see what else is there to be chosen. Every day, wake up and set the intention, "May I consciously choose what is choosing me, and may I say thank you to how the creations that are choosing me make me a brighter and better version of myself, even if it's creating the space to admit how much I don't like doing this. May I be honest, may I be honorable, may I say thank you, and may I choose what is choosing me." And with this, you will come to see you don't have to endure the hardship of sacrifice. You'll actually allow the situation to be a doorway into eternal freedom.

---

*Do you feel different levels of love? Are there different vibrations of love?*

---

Sure, there are different vibrations of love. There's personal love, romantic love, parental love, sibling love, friendship love, and there's love that we feel from spirit. The higher we go in vibration, the more intense the love.

The higher you go, the more potent the love is as a creator of reality. When love is high enough in vibration, it's not just two hearts satisfying one another. It's new worlds being created by their lights merging as one.

When we talk about paths like tantra, lovemaking becomes a very sacred, intentional, spiritual way of accessing higher dimensional realities. This comprehension and the process of honoring connection—physical, emotional, spiritual—becomes a gateway into unity with the Divine.

There are levels to love. The higher the vibration, the more pure and the more potent a healer it becomes for ourselves and those we love. But the highest levels can only be accessed through various levels of integrity and conduct, which is part of the checks and balances of the Universe.

---

*"Can you please offer help with panic attacks and fear?"*

---

When these feelings arise, first, say to yourself, "I accept that this fear and panic is only here to be loved."

Second, and this can be all you have to do when your feelings are just too overwhelming to say those words, simply have a seat somewhere, preferably somewhere private, and slowly count from one to ten. Then, count slowly backwards from ten back to one. And then, just feel.

As you count, you'll feel everything relax. Your nervous system will go into a state of regulation. You may feel a part of you wants to count faster. That's just anxiety trying to move you beyond the moment faster than the moment is being resolved. Anxiety wants you to exceed the speed limit of consciousness!

Count slowly to ten, then ten back to one. Allow yourself to pull back from a future possibility as you remain in the present moment. Do not rush through the moment faster than it's meant to be experienced.

---

*Profound, Matt! I'm feeling deep gratitude to you for all that's been shared.*

---

I just want to say to everyone who may ever experience this transmission, thank you for your presence and participation. Thank you for being alive on the planet at this time. Thank you for shining your light, even if what you focus and fixate on may be how shut down you feel.

Just by being alive on the planet right now, during one of the most intense and tumultuous times in recorded history—*just by being alive*—you are bringing light to this planet. You are embodying a vibrational frequency. As an individual, unique and unlike anyone else in history, you're bringing to this planet a vibration that has never been known before and will never be known again.

No matter what you're personally doing with your choices, whether uplifting and loving yourself or getting down on yourself, it doesn't change the fact that you are fulfilling the highest mission of the Universe: to deliver to this world—wherever you walk and however you breathe—a unique vibrational frequency that only you can bring.

I am here. I'm with you. I see you. I bow in your presence. It is you who I serve, and I serve you in the name of love.

I love you.

---

*To find out more about Matt, his books, and his channeling, please visit Matt's website at www.mattkahn.org.*

---

# Chapter 5

## Developing the Gifts of Healing, Channeling, and Light Language *with Daniel Scranton*

### About Daniel

Daniel is a trance channel, spiritual teacher, and sound healer. He's been channeling the 12th-dimensional, non-physical collective known as The Creators since the fall of 2010. Since then, a wide array of other guides and collectives have spoken through him. Some of those include Archangel Michael, Archangel Gabriel, Quan Yin, Yeshua, The Hathors, The Pleiadian High Council of Seven, and The Arcturian Council. He also channels light languages and healing overtones, has written six books, including his acclaimed series, *Ascension: The Shift to the Fifth Dimension*.

### The Four Cornerstones of The 9D Arcturian Council Teachings

---

*Aloha, Daniel! So happy you're with us! Please tell us where you are right now.*

---

Here I am! I'm on Mount Haleakalā in Maui, known by some as the heart chakra of planet Earth.

*Somebody's got to live there. Not a bad gig. Nice manifesting! Please share with us the main teachings you channel from the Arcturians.*

Their emphasis has always been on acceptance, forgiveness, compassion, and unconditional love. Those four aspects of life are, I believe, everyone's purpose here and everyone's mission. Purpose and mission, contrary to popular thinking, have little to do with our line of work or career.

Work and career have a place, but we all still have family life, friends, and people who bug us. We all have the things that come into our experience and make us feel certain things—that's the real work. That's what it's all about. And by addressing these four things, we ascend—by doing *that* work on ourselves. Everything else is for the purpose of having those opportunities.

Acceptance, forgiveness, compassion, and unconditional love. I do believe that's the right order to go in as well, because you can't just say, "I'm going to forgive everybody," without first asking, "Do I accept that it happened? Do I acknowledge my participation in the cocreation of it?" Because if you don't, if you maintain victimhood status, it's hard to say, "Okay. I forgive that person or those people."

*Excellent and compelling. Shall we bring them on?*

## The 9D Arcturian Council Message

We are very excited to be here with all of you. We are with you at all times. We have agreed to be available for you at this time in your spiritual evolution on planet Earth. We knew that you would need some assistance with the evolution of your consciousness, and you knew that you would need that assistance as well. We are available to each and every one of you, twenty-four hours a day. Any time you need us, any request you want to make: we have the ability to focus on myriad places all at once and not dilute ourselves in any way. We are not in any way diminished by the multitasking that we do when we answer more than one person's call at a time. So you may call upon us at any time.

Some of you may find that you are capable of channeling us, and we welcome that. We welcome anyone who wants to connect with us. We are very interested in anchoring more Arcturian energy to planet Earth and adding more of our teachings to the conversation that is going on here at this time in the spiritual and New Age communities.

We are very interested in the awakening process for all of you, as well as all the by-products or side effects of awakening that help you ultimately ascend and become your fifth dimensional higher selves. That is the ultimate goal in *this lifetime* for everyone. Ascension is available to all who are on the planet right now.

## Developing the Gifts of Healing, Channeling, and Light Language

### Being Awake

We would like to start by giving you our definition of what it means to be awake. We know that awakening can mean a lot of different things to a lot of different people. Our definition of being awake is that you know with every fiber of your being that you are Source Energy in the flesh and so is everyone else on Earth, throughout the galaxy, throughout the universe, throughout the multiverse, throughout all existence. Everything and everyone is pure Source.

There is nothing outside of Source. Source used Source to create every single one of us. We are all composed of Source. We don't just have a little bit of Source inside ourselves; *everything* is Source. Everything is composed of the same Source stuff. When you come to that realization, it becomes possible for you to start to live your life accordingly.

To see others as Source no matter what they are doing, no matter what they are saying, and no matter what they are believing is an important step in the process, because there is no separation in reality between you and any other that you are experiencing, no matter what.

Now, you may wonder, "How can that be the case?" This might

prevent certain people from awakening because they have challenging experiences with others. They've been hurt by others, or they've seen others do horrible things to humans or to animals: people who don't care at all about how their business affects the environment, people who would drop bombs and start wars, and people who would be verbally abusive. How can any of those people represent Source or be in any way an aspect of Source Energy? To answer that question, we need to go back to the beginning.

## How Did This All Get Started?

In the beginning, there was Source, and Source wanted to know Itself. To do that, Source had to create individuated conscious beings who could have certain experiences and who could go to different parts of Source to have those different experiences. This created the idea, or the illusion, of separation between individuals, and made it necessary to have physical bodies. It also became necessary to have a forgetting process that would allow people to have certain experiences or to be certain beings—ETs included—that you can only have when you forget who you and everyone else really are. This is also when you start to believe in the ideas of mortality and shortages: "There's only so much to go around, and if I don't get more than my share, I might perish and no longer exist."

These are the types of beliefs that needed to be taken on by people throughout the universe to have certain experiences that they could only have within that forgetting. And in having those experiences, certain emotions were and are possible. You cannot feel a certain way unless you've forgotten who and what you really are and that you created this reality—that the reality you're experiencing is your creation. This forgetting is necessary in order for you to feel victimized and have the experience of being in the pit of despair.

What do you do, then, to get out of the pit of despair? Well, if you're awake, it's a lot easier to make that climb. But even those who have yet to awaken can come to that place where they accept that this has happened in their lives, that they had this experience with this person who was very unpleasant, realizing that if they just sit and wallow in their negative emotions forever, they could possibly spend the rest of their days in that pit, and so they want to get out. They realize that there must be a way out of this bad-feeling situation they find themselves in.

## The Journey and Meaning of Your Emotions

You will find now that most people who have done any sort of work or research on spirituality or psychology, or are in the helping professions, recognize the importance of feeling your feelings, that it's necessary for you to accept your feelings. You have to accept the situation. You have to accept the person. You have to accept yourself for being in the situation, *which does not mean blame yourself.* And you have to accept your emotions as part of the process of being human. It's part of the process of living on planet Earth and having certain experiences.

When you get to that point where you can accept and process your emotions, you can then let them go by feeling into them with every fiber of your being, with breathing into them, with embracing them, and knowing that they're finite. Understand that if you do, they will eventually dissipate. That's when you're doing the necessary work on yourself. The thing that many people don't realize is that there *is* an endpoint to the negative emotions they're feeling. They don't have to numb themselves with street drugs, alcohol, or pharmaceuticals that were prescribed. They don't have to numb themselves with shopping, gambling, sex, smoking, or any other type of addiction. Any addiction can be seen as a way of numbing oneself to pain.

When you realize that there's an endpoint to the pain you're experiencing, you're willing to go into it, feel it completely, and thereby let it go—release it—and you'll come to this place of calm, peace, and inner balance. You'll feel neutral. You don't feel great, but you feel some relief. You'll get to the point where you feel no more negativity. It's from that place where you can say to yourself, "I want to forgive this person. I want to let this go as well. I don't want to hang on to this hate," or resentment, or anger, or fear, or whatever it is you're feeling around a person or situation. It doesn't feel good. You want to let it go. You don't want to go back to the pit of despair after just having climbed out of it by processing all that really hard-to-feel emotional stuff.

Instead, you decide you're going to forgive. You say to yourself, "I forgive this act and this person." Then, maybe you come to the place where you understand that the person themself was abused or hurt in some way in their lives, they were struggling with something that was very hard for them, and they took it out on you. You might even come to a place of feeling some compassion for the person who hurt you.

Now, when you get to that point and you're able to connect to the unconditional love that you truly are, it doesn't mean that you're saying, "I love the abusive act," or, "I love the abusive words," or, "I love anything that was done or that was negative and hurtful." But you can say, "I choose to be love in the face of this, because that's who and what I really am." Therefore, when we say you understand, we mean that you are beginning to viscerally grasp that you are Source, even if only as an intellectual concept at first.

What may begin as, "Well, I get it. I get how it all works now. I've seen the studies on quantum physics, how particles respond to one another and respond to the observer, quantum entanglement—I get all that intellectually," evolves into true awakening. Awakening to the truth of who you *really* are, who you were before your forgetting—literally defining what Source is through the feeling of love.

When you really want to know yourself as Source, you want to *be* love unconditionally. When in the face of anything, no matter what's going on, no matter what's not happening (that you want to happen) in your life, you can say, "I have decided that I want to be love. It's my goal in all situations to radiate love, to respond with love, and to give others the love that perhaps they're not getting from the places they expected to get it in life." That's a very satisfying feeling, because now you're allowing Source Energy to move more fluidly to and through you.

Now, we said earlier that everything is Source; everything is composed of Source. Still, in your lives of seeming separation, you can best give yourself the experience of feeling more Source by tuning in to it when you're focused on your heart space. It's easier for you to access the portal that takes you directly to the Source Energy dimension when you're focused on the center of your heart space—the organ, the chakra, its space. Tune in to the very middle of it, and you'll feel a warm glow. You can feel a sensation of love.

### *Processing Emotions and Feeling Source Energy*

When you process negative emotions, give it your full attention and proceed with great love. Feel what you're feeling and notice where you find it in your body. Then, focus on the center of your heart; breathe into it. Feel the warm, peaceful, loving expression that is Source, and feel it expanding out, filling you up—through where the negative emotions are—filling up all your chakras and your energy field.

Getting yourself into the vibration of love is also a great way to start your day. Love is not just something you feel for a select few people in your life who are really lovable or who you're related to. You ultimately want to feel love even if the person you're with is not being lovable in every moment. Love is a state of being. It's a vibration. It's the best way we have of knowing Source and knowing ourselves as Source.

Don't wait for others to fill up your tank. Go out and be what you want to see more of in the world. You want that love to be reflected back to you. You want everyone else to know that they are Source Energy as well. It's easier to get that message across to them if you're being it rather than you telling them that they are Source, writing a book about it, or making a series of viral videos on it. You must be it instead, and then they'll feel it. They'll feel it coming off you, and they'll want to know what your secret is. They'll want to know how you seem to always exude that loving kindness, that compassion, that Source Energy bliss that comes from within you. Then, you can tell them, because they asked, because they're curious, and because it's something you're going to want to share with people.

## Supernatural Gifts and Performing Miracles

Once you do enough of this type of clearing and activating work, you're likely to stumble upon some spiritual gifts and abilities that come to you because you're offering a higher vibration. All the things that you can see with clairvoyance, hear with clairaudience, all the things you can channel, all the healing energies you can run through you, and all the information that you can gather with psychic and intuitive abilities—all of it's there all the time, around each and every one of you, but you've got to tune in to it by offering a higher vibration.

When you raise your vibration, suddenly you have a greater awareness. You have an awareness of things you couldn't tune in to before.

One of the lovely side effects of being awake is this tuning in. Usually, it starts in a way where you don't even realize that tuning in is what you're doing. One of the things we often see in those who are beginning to tap into their gifts is that they're having a sensation, they're having electrical impulses moving through them, they're feeling heat, they're moving involuntarily or twitching, and they begin speaking light language without even knowing what light language is or ever having heard of it. They feel warm sensations in the palms of their hands. They don't really know what to do in these scenarios, and some people even feel that it might be a negative experience because they didn't ask for it. They weren't saying, "Let me summon this feeling of energy surging through my body right now." But even though they didn't ask, it starts happening.

Some people might even think, "Well, this must be a psychic attack. This must be a negative entity attachment." It's important not to jump to that conclusion when something is happening to you that's unexpected or unexplainable. Instead, you want to assume that it's good: that it's a good thing that's happening, that it's taking you to a higher level of consciousness, that you're accessing your spiritual gifts and abilities, that you want to run with it and keep doing whatever you were doing that got you to that place.

For a lot of you who are awake, you realize the significance of meditation. You realize that meditation is a very important part of your spiritual evolution, of you having inner peace, of you being able to process emotions, and of you even being aware of your thoughts and emotions. Meditation can be a hugely important practice for all of you.

In meditation, for example, you might discover that these sorts of twitches, heat sensations, involuntary movements, and energy surges start happening even though you didn't sit and say, "Today I'm going to meditate, and hopefully, I'll start channeling some higher dimensional consciousness."

This is something that happens to a lot of people. If you can go with it, just lean in; it can develop into more. It's you becoming aware, in a visceral way, that you've tapped into some energy that you weren't previously tapping into during your normal waking state, or even when you were resting, healing, or meditating. That's what happened to Daniel here. That's what clued him in that perhaps he was going to channel someday. It was involuntary movements while he was performing Reiki on people.

When these types of things start happening, follow them and see where they may lead. Say, "Well, I'm going to keep doing *this* because when I do, I'm tapping into something more than just the traditional resting, healing, or meditating energy that someone else normally has when they're doing these things."

A lot of people have such experiences, whether or not they meditate, but they don't necessarily realize that those experiences meant they're tapping into their spiritual gifts. Therefore, they didn't keep going with it.

## *Getting Started and Energizing Your Gifts*

Now, a few things can really help when you want to tap into your spiritual gifts:

> *One: Consistency.* Do what you're doing on a regular basis. Once a day would be ideal.
>
> *Two: Get happy.* Have some sort of practice getting into the state of a higher consciousness, a higher vibration, before you sit to access your spiritual gift. You want the lead into it to be something that's fun, something you just love to do, something that puts you into a state of alignment. Then, sit down and tap in.
>
> *Three: Trust what you receive.* Once you start accessing whatever you're accessing, there's a tendency on the part of most people to doubt it, and say, "Well, that was probably just me. That seems very similar to what I heard so-and-so experiencing. I don't know if I'm any good at this. I don't feel like I'm tapping into all the answers that could ever possibly be known."
>
> *Four: Don't compare your gifts to those of others.* People also say, for example, "Well, I do healing on people, I feel energy, but I'm not getting a lot of information. When so-and-so treated me, they spoke about all the things they saw and all the things they heard. I'm not getting that when I do my healing, so I must not be doing it right, or I must not have the gift that others have for healing." They stop or sell themselves short instead of considering that where that other person is, is where they're headed. If you just compare yourself to others, who've likely been doing it for many years, you'll never give yourself the chance to get to where that person is—in probably far less time, given the rising energies on the planet right now.
>
> *Five: Share your gifts.* Give them a place to go. Be the instrument of their flow. The more spiritual gifts and abilities you

find and share, the more you'll tap into and the more gifts will come. More will flow to you and through you because you're giving those energies a place to go, an exit point. You can even do healings, for example, on your pets or on the people who you live with. You can talk to people who live thousands of miles away, and say, "Hey, would you like me to do a distance healing on you? Can I help you with anything that you're working on right now?" You don't have to wait until people line up at your door. It's up to you to be proactive so that you can gain and build upon your experiences. Then, once you get the positive feedback that will naturally come your way, you'll find the confidence to keep going with it.

These are things that a lot of you will just need to work through as you tap into your gifts. Face that self-doubt, process the fear of exposure, the fear that people will laugh at you, or that you'll be ostracized by your community—all things that likely happened in your past lives that you're afraid will happen in this life.

You're not going to be burned at the stake in this lifetime for accessing your spiritual gifts. In fact, today you're more likely to get your own reality television show. Now is a much different time, though you're not necessarily going to get everyone's approval for doing it, and some people are going to think that it's actually bad that you're doing it. But you have to be willing to do it anyway in order to be true to yourself, to anchor in more of that positive energy, and to bring the world more of what you want to see in it.

Tuning in to your spiritual gifts is a very important aspect of the awakening process. As you continue exploring and discovering your unique gifts, even though you're not yet where you want to be, understand that with desire and consistency *you will get there.* You'll get there through baby steps, gradually becoming more adept at whatever it is you're doing.

By moving forward with your abilities, you'll give the world that gift and see it reflected back to you, which is a beautiful experience. Everyone has things they would like to see differently in the world, and this is how you can be a part of that process.

As you continue with your awakening, you'll also recognize that your sensitivity is a gift. Your ability to tap into compassion is a gift.

Your willingness to feel your emotions is a gift. Your empathy is a gift. These are not flashy. They don't get you a lot of attention. People may not even agree with you that these are gifts, but they truly are the gifts that will help you become a better creator of your reality. Because if you're willing to feel one thing, even if it's unpleasant, then you're opening the floodgates to feeling everything, including all positive emotions as well.

You want to create using positive energy and high vibrations, and that's what sensitivity, compassion, and empathy represent, just like positive thoughts and positive actions. They will powerfully help you create a better experience of reality for yourself and for others.

## Tapping into Your Chakra System

If, however, your sensitivity makes you feel like you have to hide inside, away from people, it's important you process your fear, by first identifying it. Find where it sits in your chakra system. Breathe into it until it's no longer there. When you reach that place of balance, calm, and peaceful neutrality, then you can tap into what you actually want to feel because it will be right there, maybe in your heart or in one of your other chakras.

Experiment and have fun moving your conscious awareness up and down your chakras, saying, "All right, I know love is accessible to me in my heart, and I can focus there to feel it, breathing into it, but what about joy? Where does joy sit in my chakra system? Where's confidence? Where's vitality? Where's abundance? Where's freedom? Where's peace?" Simply explore where each of these sits within you so that you can more easily tap into them when you want to.

Or take your consciousness straight to the solar plexus chakra and turn on your self-confidence vibration—really get it flowing. You can even envision your chakras with an inner guitar string or cord of energy that stretches from their top to their bottom, right down the middle. Imagine you're reaching in, and you're plucking the string and getting it vibrating. Then, you feel it, your confidence building and building.

Confidence doesn't have to be based on something you did or praise you received from someone else. It can just be something you want to feel or something you want to activate. It's not a cocky confidence; it's not arrogant. It's a confidence that comes from knowing who you really are as Source Energy, while knowing everyone else is Source Energy too. This kind of confidence is not putting you above anyone else.

## Ascension Symptoms

So, what are ascension symptoms? Often, they appear as unexpected experiences in the body that can't be explained and that doctors don't have a name for. People tend to have these symptoms when they're tapping into energy while there's still some resistance.

As we were describing before, you may start accessing some of your gifts and abilities, getting some downloads, and finding energy running through you that you're also thwarting. You go into fear mode, resistant to the flow, and so you experience fatigue, headaches, indigestion, and neck or back pain.

These are classic ascension symptoms that a lot of people are now experiencing. When you have an ascension symptom, it's wise to acknowledge it as such, and to ask, "Is there some resistance I can release that will help these energies flow more? Is there some emotion I need to process to thereby release my symptoms?"

Of course, you're going to want to take really good care of your physical body once you realize that it's a vehicle for high frequency energies. You'll want to stay hydrated and get plenty of sleep and rest. You're probably going to feel attracted to lighter foods that carry a naturally higher vibration. If you've ever grown food yourself, picked and eaten it right out of the ground, you'll understand what we mean by food having a certain vibration because you can feel and taste it. Those are the foods you're going to be more attracted to. Fresh, local, organic, and natural in the sense that you won't have to do a lot to it prior to consumption. You won't have to add a lot of salad dressing and salt and things to make it more palatable because you'll recognize that it's wonderful just as it is. This is what you'll be drawn to because you'll be operating at a higher vibration, only wanting that which is going to feel light in your body.

You don't have to go from omnivore to vegan all at once, but you'll begin wanting more fruits, vegetables, seeds, and nuts in your system. Then, the energies will run through you better, and you'll find greater ease accessing higher frequency thoughts. You'll refrain from putting in your body a lot of other energies that have to be sifted through to get what you actually want. You'll actually be consuming the energies your chakras want to be receiving.

A lot of people find that as they awaken, they also want to try new things. But like we said, just because you're awake doesn't mean you have to go to extremes or do all the things that everyone else seems to be doing in the New Age. You don't have to become polyamorous and join a spiritual community and put everything into cryptocurrency and have ayahuasca journeys. You don't have to do anything that doesn't feel like it's aligned for you or isn't something that you truly want to do.

You have something else that's a gift and superpower within you called *discernment*. Everyone needs it right now because there's so much being put out there on the internet in this age of information. Everyone needs to use their discernment to decide whether an idea feels right to them—whether it's something that rings true and resonates with them.

That's another reason it's good to be focusing on your heart, because your heart has that ability to tell you how something feels, whereas your mind could certainly talk you into it and say, "Well, a lot of people seem to believe this is true, and I like that person who believes it, and so it makes sense for me." But when you have to talk yourself into something, chances are you're not paying attention to what you're feeling in your gut that knows, "This is not for me." You don't have to drink the Kool-Aid on this one. You can pass and say, "You know what, I think I'm going to shut my computer off for a while and meditate or spend time in nature or spend time with my pet—doing things that actually feel good to me that are all very spiritual but that don't require a whole new set of beliefs about what's going on in the world."

There's a lot that can distract you from your own awakening, including people who tell you, "Well, you're not awake unless you know this to be true." That's not our definition of being awake. It's not about information. It's about knowing who you really are and who everyone else really is. All else you can take with a grain of salt. You can decide what feels good to you and what spiritual practices you want to partake in.

If something new really does call you to it, then perhaps it's an experience you would benefit from. But ultimately, you simply want to be able to go within yourself to have any mystical, magical, multidimensional experience. You want to be able to access a higher vibration even if you're sitting in your apartment in a city somewhere, without ingesting stimulants, far from a place like Mount Haleakalā or any place where someone else might find that it's easier to tap into higher frequency energies.

As this becomes your new normal, as you realize you have everything inside of you because you're an infinite and eternal being—that it all exists within you, the entire world, the entire universe—then, going "out there" to have certain experiences doesn't have to be done; they don't have to be had in order for you to feel tapped in. You can tap into the pyramids by going inside of yourself, or you can tap into Stonehenge by going inside of yourself; you'll find that they all exist inside of you. You have access to them all the time.

That's the place you want to get to in your awakening: to know that whatever is "out there" is also "in here." And whatever I cannot do that's out there right now, I can do by focusing inside, by focusing on the vast and infinite array of experiences and vibrations that are available to me at all times when I focus inwardly.

Have as many experiences, inwardly or outwardly, as you want to have because experience is also what it's all about. As we said in the beginning, Source wanted to experience Itself and still does. That's why all the possibilities for different experiences exist. That's where creation comes in. Part of being awake is realizing that you are a creator being. *You create your reality.* You create what you experience. You create it all. It's all a projection from within you, and everything you experience is your projection. When other souls are involved, it's cocreation. They agree to be there for you, as you agree to be there for them.

## Living Deliberately and Manifesting Consciously

Now, a lot of people can get very excited right away about knowing that they create their reality, and then they tend to think about all the things they want—all the things they want to create and all the things they want to experience. If it doesn't happen right away, or even within six months, then those people can get very discouraged, put their vision boards away, and give up on dreaming their way into a better-feeling reality, going back to working at things and taking lots of actions and logically trying to figure everything out.

What we would like for people to do instead is to realize that all that time you spend focusing on what it is you want, whether it's a partner, a new car, a vacation, or a home, is time well spent. It's time you spent feeling good. You were pure in those moments, offering your vibration in the focusing on the desired outcome or the desired set of circumstances. You were pure until you started to say, "Wait a minute, I've been doing this now for six days in a row, and I still haven't seen any evidence that it's working."

What we recommend is that you simply make your wishes known once. You can tell the Universe *once* what you want, vibrate in harmony with it once, put it out there, let it go, and then go live your life. *Go do the things that are available to you, that you can do, that make you happy, and that take your mind off the fact that this or that hasn't manifested yet.* You'll be doing yourself a great service because you'll be opening up.

There's a process in manifestation that many people overlook called *receiving*. You're more likely to receive what you've asked for when you're doing something you love: when you're meditating, relaxing, focusing on a sunset, petting your pet, or whatever you're happiest doing. Then, you're open. Then, you're relaxed. You're not worrying about whether it's going to come, when it's going to come, and what it's going to look like when it does come. You're not thinking about any of that, because you already have certainty that you create your reality and that whatever you put out there already exists in that moment you think of it, so all you have to do is relax, live your life, and be the person you want to be. You don't have to be anyone else.

You don't have to pretend. You don't have to recite certain ritualistic statements over and over again or have the right crystals. Just trust, live your life, and continue. Then the Universe will continue to bring you more and more of these beautiful awakening experiences that ultimately help all of you ascend.

*Earlier, you said ascension to the fifth dimension is everyone's goal at this time. Can you explain the fifth dimension? What will that mean for us to ascend into the fifth dimension?*

It's a higher level of consciousness that represents a higher vibration. So, you'll exist in a higher frequency of vibration that will allow you to have new experiences you couldn't have in the third and fourth dimensions. Again, it's all about Source being able to experience Itself, and your experiences are part of this.

Once you've had all the third and fourth dimensional experiences, and you've accepted, forgiven, and gotten past anything that you've been resisting or judging, letting all that go, then your consciousness naturally rises to a higher vibrational state. This allows you to have new experiences of yourself, others, the galaxy, form, and energy. You have instant manifestations. You have a light body. You're able to go wherever you want to go.

Money is not an issue because you're creating everything and manifesting it instantaneously. Health is not a problem anymore because you have a light body that you can shapeshift into whatever you want it to be, including whatever level of health and vitality you want to have. Relationships are not a problem because you realize that everyone is Source, they realize that you're Source, and you both realize that we're all creating everything together. So, you don't have the issues you now have with people, money, jealousy, and other things like these, because you simply left those levels of consciousness behind as you rose up to the fifth dimension of consciousness.

*Is that within our reach within this incarnation? To live at a fifth dimensional level where we really have transcended everything through acceptance, forgiveness, and unconditional love?*

It is your destiny.

*In this incarnation? As in, we're going to start seeing this amongst ourselves? I would imagine somebody's going to be the first out there to be seen doing something supernatural, and then we'll see it done more and more. Is that really on the horizon—the immediate horizon?*

You're already seeing it. So many people are tapping into their spiritual gifts and abilities. You're seeing so many people channeling, speaking light language, healing, and accessing their psychic gifts. You're already seeing what it looks like when someone taps into higher consciousness.

Everything else is coming, but don't be in a hurry to get there. Enjoy where you are right now. Enjoy the experiences that are available to you right now because there's so much within them for you. Otherwise, it's like saying, "Well, I'm going to skip over all these flavors of ice cream, because I just want to get to the one over there."

*Is it safe to assume that everyone partaking in this transmission is probably operating in the fourth dimension because of their attunement to this kind of information? That they've attracted this material to themselves for its cocreation?*

You made the transition to the fourth dimension on December 21, 2012, and you've had access to fifth dimensional energies ever since. You also have the choice of staying in the lower vibrations of third dimensional egoic mentality. Each person has that option. That's why you see such a wide array of experiences all across the planet today. But not everybody knows they have the ability to tap into new energies yet. Those who do are going to help spread that love and the higher vibrations around so that the effect is felt throughout the whole multiverse.

We love what Bashar has said about how when you change yourself, you don't actually change the world you're living on; instead, you shift yourself to another world and another world and another world. But we'd like to add that for your *every* single thought, emotion, intention, and action, you really do change the entire multiverse. You affect all realities and all universes because you're spreading more positivity out into the collective consciousness.

There's a universal collective consciousness. There's a human collective consciousness. There's a galactic collective consciousness. There's the Source collective consciousness. So, you do affect everything. Whenever you do, say, or think something positive—whenever you love—you are adding something to the whole that could only come through you.

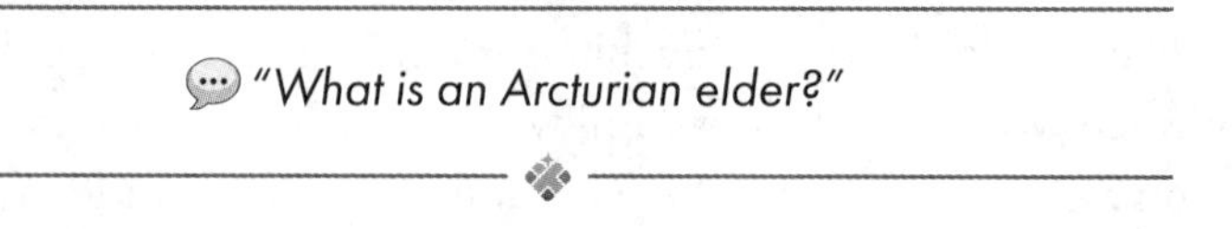

*"What is an Arcturian elder?"*

There are many beings who have lived in our star system who have taken on physical form, although we're mostly nonphysical or in a higher dimensional range. But there have been those who have taken on bodies and incarnated to be your teachers, healers, and leaders—who set an example of what is possible.

An elder in our system is one who has lived in the physical for a long time, just like you do on Earth, thereby gaining a lot more experience and wisdom to share, compared to someone who is, say, dropping in for the first time. Of course, you want to have those who are wise, like the elders, to learn from much more quickly.

*Are you Arcturian elders that are channeling through Daniel?*

We're a nonphysical collective, and so we don't really have age. Therefore, you could call us an elder. People call us grandparents. People call us all kinds of things. We are a consciousness and a collective who wants to serve, help, heal, and activate. We can be so much to so many when we are let in.

*"If you could say one thing to those of us who can feel our gifts developing but aren't quite there yet, what would it be? And what was the final thing that enabled Daniel to fully open up and channel?"*

You're perfect right where you are. Your degree of tapping into your gifts is giving you that experience right now. It may not feel like you're at that master level yet, but there is something for you within where you are right now. As you embrace it and accept it, you'll feel like this is your journey: "Now I get to grow. Now I get to experience what it feels like to go from where I am to the next level and the next level and the next level, and that's fun and interesting and unique. I'm so glad I get to have this experience." That's what we would say to all of you who are starting out.

Daniel was "lucky" in a sense that he had helpers. He had Abraham [channeled by Esther Hicks], who encouraged him at an event. He had Bashar, with whom he spoke about channeling with. He had Nora Herold, who helped him immensely in gaining more confidence in what he was doing.

Being told by Abraham that he was going to channel was a life-altering experience for Daniel, because he didn't know what was happening to him. He didn't know why he was experiencing all the things he was experiencing. And he didn't think that what he was doing was necessarily the right thing to do. But just getting that little nudge and being told "this is something you're going to do, keep at it" was what he needed to hear. Then, he just needed to sit more, tune in more, and eventually get to the place where all the herky-jerky, involuntary movements and weird facial contortions became words—words that he was able to express verbally for the first time. It just took him sitting and doing that time and time again, for about forty-five minutes to an hour each time, before, eventually, he was able to form the words.

*"So many young people are dying by suicide because the world is struggling. How do I help my daughter who has decided at age twenty-three to end her own life?"*

These experiences where you get to the point of feeling suicidal can be major breakthroughs. Obviously, those who follow through and complete the task of taking their own lives have a path that involves not being in their bodies anymore. It is very sad for those who are left behind, mourning the loss of their loved one. But for someone like your daughter, know that she's on the precipice of something here, that there's a breakthrough that can come when someone hits that rock bottom and gets to the point where they feel like they want to take their own life and to leave this world with all its pain.

Daniel reached that point in March of 2010. The very next night, after he really thought about how he would leave this world, was when he had the most amazing experience of his life. That's when energies flooded his body from head to toe, over and over. It was like a near-death experience for him.

You can, as a mother, look for more evidence of people who hit that rock bottom, experienced suicidal thoughts, and the turnaround that came out of it, to make yourself feel better right now. As far as your daughter is concerned, you can normalize the experience for her. Let her know that many people reach a point at some time in their lives, thinking, "I'd just rather not be here experiencing any of this."

Also send her transmissions of love from your heart. Surround her with your love that you can access from within. Of course, it's hard to access love for someone when you're worried about them or when you're afraid of what they might do. But that's your work right now. Your work is to go through the experience, allow those emotions, and get to that calm place and say, "What do I actually want to feel around my daughter? I want to feel that love I felt when I held her in my arms for the very first time, send it out like a beam of light from the center of my chest to her, and surround her in that love and light. I want to send the message out that she is loved, that there is love available to her, and that she can join me in this vibration of love if she wants to."

---

*"Can you give us practical steps to develop or receive our soul's gifts or to tap into abilities we've had in other lifetimes to benefit our current lives?"*

---

Yes, indeed. Well, first of all, every day that you wake up, you can tell the Universe, "I'm ready, open, and willing to receive all the energies that are available to me that are coming from higher dimensions, higher frequency beings and collectives, and beings of the light. I'm open to running those energies through my body." Because first and foremost, when it comes to spiritual gifts, you want to feel something. You want to feel something different. You want to feel tapped in, like you're plugged into something.

You can access those energies if you set out to do so every day. Put yourself in a position where it's easier for you to do so. Maybe sit under a tree. Sit on a nice patch of grass. Go to a very calm, serene part of your home that you set up as your sanctuary, where you can sit and do this. But give yourself that experience of just receiving, and eventually, what you receive will fill you up so much that it will want to then burst forth from you in some way. If it's a clairvoyant or clairaudient experience, you'll be able to interpret that energy in such a way that it makes sense to you and it makes sense to others.

---

*"Is speaking in tongues and speaking in light language the same thing? What are the benefits to me or others in using light language?"*

---

They are the exact same thing. Light languages contain within them a vibration, an energy, galactic light codes, sacred geometry, activations, and healing potentials. What they contain runs the gamut. And you get to decide before you start what you want the light language to be about for you, for that person, for humanity, for a group of people, or for whomever you've decided you want to send that light language out to. Just set the intention, then let the light language come through, knowing that it's holding that intention and sending out the energy that's going to give the person exactly what it is they need.

---

*"Why is it that we feel more connected and emotionally attracted to, or resonate with, some people over others?"*

---

You have longer histories together. You have these packs that you travel in called *soul groups* or *soul families*, and you have experience after experience after experience with each other, not always the same. You're not always the father and the other person's not always the child, or the mother and the child. Sometimes it's reversed. Sometimes you're cousins; sometimes you're friends.

But you have all these experiences with these other souls that make them light up to you and you light up to them. Most of the time it's mutual when it's a soul family member that you're in contact with. They fit like a glove. They just feel right to you. You know that there's something that the two of you are going to do together or are going to feel in each other's presence, and you want more of that. And so, you start making arrangements to get together.

Of course, with family members that feeling is built in because you're related to them. With family members, you tend to give each other a hard time. You have most of your troubles with family members because you want to love that person so much, and they're doing whatever they tend to do to make it challenging for you to do so. But in most cases, you're not just going to write them off or out of your life. You're going to keep them in your life and keep discovering the love that you are, in spite of your differences or the hurt that's already happened between the two of you. You want so much to love that person that you're willing to keep going with the relationship in spite of the fact that a lot of bad blood may exist between you.

---

*"Since all our lives are happening at once, is being able to access past or other lives a channeling experience?"*

---

It is a channeling experience. *Channeling is basically you tuning in to something.* So, it's accurate to say that everyone's channeling all the time because you're always tapped into something. You're either tapped into a thought stream or a soul fragment, or you're tapped into the energy of a room you just walked into.

When you don't set your dial on the station you want to be on, then you're just channeling randomly. Or you're channeling the same thing as yesterday because nothing changed in the environment or nothing changed within you.

When you're channeling with intention, you're saying, "This is what I want to set my vibration to harmonize with, connect to, become one with, merge with, and then have an experience with."

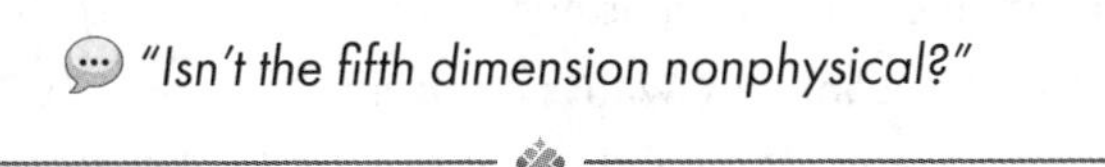

*"Isn't the fifth dimension nonphysical?"*

It is not. The way that *we* break down the universe is into twelve dimensions; the first nonphysical dimension is the ninth dimension, where we are. The fifth, sixth, and seventh dimensions are all physical.

By our scale, the eighth dimension is a transitional dimension, like the fourth is for you now. The eighth dimension helps you to transition into a nonphysical being totally and completely.

*Can you please explain densities, as opposed to dimensions?*

When people break the universe down into densities, they're usually only seven, whereas we're on a twelve-point dimension scale. So, of course, sixth *density* is going to be different from sixth *dimension*. Sixth density would be nonphysical.

*"In what ways, if any, is the transformation to a vegan way of eating and living a fundamental imperative for the awakening of humanity?"*

We're glad you asked the question. When you awaken you tend to become more compassionate. You tend to look at the world differently. You tend to look at plants, animals, the Earth—everything—differently. There's more love flowing through you. And so there's more of a likelihood that you're going to say, "You know what, I don't want to eat anything that once breathed or had eyes." You just come to that naturally. That's why certain people make that choice. But you don't have to make that choice in order to awaken.

*"What's blocking all of us humans from becoming channels? And as channels, what's our greatest responsibility to others as we use it not only for ourselves but for others?"*

The greatest block comes from a belief that there's something special about a person who channels. But there's nothing special about Daniel here. Trust us, Daniel was thirty-eight years old and did not feel special when he started channeling; he didn't feel like he was someone who always knew things or was always tapped in, and he had a very traditional upbringing. He was raised Catholic, went to church every Sunday, feared God, all of that; he didn't have any spiritual experiences whatsoever. Yet somehow, he was able to get past that block.

If you believe that it's possible to channel, then you're willing to do what it takes to tap in. You're willing to take the time to do it. You're willing to put forth the right frequency and to raise your vibration enough to reach that level of consciousness. Once you do start channeling, yes, it's important to check with yourself and ask, "All rright, was that just me putting something out there that I believe in? Was I overly influencing what I was getting?"

The vast majority of people who are channeling have a genuine desire to be of service and not to manipulate or put forth negative or false information, although whatever the channeler is focusing on in their non-channeling state is going to filter, or color, what they bring through while channeling.

As a channeler, your responsibility is to keep focusing on that which is positive, integrated, and enlightening—bringing people together and raising the level of consciousness—and not on all the divisive stuff that's out there.

*Very, very good! We've had an amazing session. Thank you so much for your sharing, your transparency, and your huge heart.*

Very good. It's been a pleasure and an honor for us as well. We are the Arcturian Council and we have enjoyed communicating with you.

*To find out more about Daniel, his books, and The 9D Arcturian Council, please visit his website at www.danielscranton.com.*

# Chapter 6

## The Self-Realization Tool Kit: Everything You Need to Raise Your Vibration

*with Darryl Anka*

### About Darryl

For forty years, people from all over the globe have made the journey to experience renowned channel Darryl Anka as he brings through a remarkable being from the future known as Bashar. Bashar is a physical ET who shares some of the most riveting, insightful, piercing ideas that clearly explain in detail how the universe works and how each person creates the reality they experience. He gives audiences the information necessary to apply these teachings so that they work to change their lives and create the reality they desire.

In addition to channeling Bashar, Darryl expresses his creative talents in the forms of writing, directing, and producing films through his own production company, Zia Films.

### Darryl's Thoughts on Open (Extraterrestrial) Contact

*Welcome, Darryl. This is such an honor. Given your many years "shocking and awing" your audiences, is there anything in Bashar's message that's now receiving a greater emphasis in the last few years, or has it always been pretty consistent?*

Hi, Mike. Great to be here. Thank you for having us.

Well, the message has had a constant aspect to it about our own ascension, but more and more, it also prepares us for a time when there will be open contact with extraterrestrial beings that he tells us is on our horizon. The spiritual "toolkits," formulas, and principles he shares are to raise our vibration to the point where we are capable of actually inviting in other beings from other civilizations, ensuring that we are capable of handling those interactions.

The intention of this open contact messaging is to remind us of who we really are—to expand our abilities, to help us interact with our galactic family, and to create more options for how we experience reality. Enabling us to expand our awareness of who we truly are.

Bashar describes himself as a "first contact specialist" of a large alliance out among the stars comprising different civilizations. His teachings, again, offer training to get us ready to join our galactic family in the years to come, finally learning that we're not just an isolated species. It's time for us to awaken.

---

*Is it fair to say that the vast majority of, if not all, ETs that might visit us are benevolent and probably further advanced spiritually than us? And that they're here to help us navigate this time of intense change, since they evidently went through their own awakening long ago and are now gallivanting the cosmos?*

Yes. Although they may have gone through some different things, they do understand what we're going through—what we're experiencing here on Earth—especially because Bashar and many other civilizations are also physical beings. So, they understand our needs in physical reality.

Bashar has expressed that while there may be negative entities out among the cosmos, the beings concerned with our evolution are assisting us by acting as a screen or a filter, keeping us from the ones that don't necessarily have our best interests at heart. The ones here, now, in contact with us, are benevolent—helping us up the ladder, so to speak.

*All right, I think we're ready. Are you comfortable now, Darryl? Ready to channel Bashar?*

Absolutely. We'll bring Bashar through and have him say what he's going to say.

## The Self-Realization Tool Kit: Everything You Need to Raise Your Vibration

We're honored to deliver information that, in our experience, when applied precisely, will help you create realities you each prefer.

We'll deliver four ideas—four principles—each with several parts. Do not be overwhelmed by this. For those who are familiar with us, it will be an opportunity to practice using these principles more precisely in your life to get stronger results. For those who are new to our information, allow yourself simply to relax and absorb. It will work for you in whatever way, shape, or form it is supposed to, synchronistically. So, just let it in, ponder it, find out what works for you, and apply as you wish.

### The Five Universal Laws

We will begin with the first part, which we call the Five Universal Laws. Now, we understand that you are familiar with the idea, to some degree, of physical laws of the so-called universe, which we perceive as a multiverse. But the idea is that even the laws you recognize as the laws of physics can change from reality to reality and universe to universe.

The five laws we are describing are truly universal in the sense that they apply to everyone, everywhere, throughout creation and parallel realities (other universes notwithstanding). These form the basic structure of existence itself.

*The Five Universal Laws*

1. You Exist
2. Everything Is Here and Now
3. The One Is the All and the All Are the One

4. What You Put Out Is What You Get Back
5. Everything Changes except the Laws

### *You Exist*

Now, this may seem very simplistic, but think about it for a moment. Existence is your natural state. It is your basic, fundamental quality. If you exist, you cannot cease to exist, because nonexistence, by definition, doesn't exist. That's its quality. The quality of nonexistence is to not exist. Therefore, what exists cannot become nonexistent.

In a sense, you could say there is no room in nonexistence for that which exists. The idea here is to not worry; you will never cease to exist. You will change your form or your perspective, but you cannot cease to exist as the unique aspect of All-That-Is—of creation—that you are.

*You Exist* is the first law, and there's nothing you can do to change that.

### *Everything Is Here and Now*

All things exist in the same moment, so to speak . Time and space are illusional projections of consciousness that allow you to experience things in a particular way, to discover new things about yourself by imposing this concept, or framework, of space and time on your consciousness. This allows you to discover new things about yourself through forgetting who you were and experiencing the playing out of processes over time and through space that give you different perspectives—allowing you to discover yourself from a new point of view. But they are illusional projections nonetheless.

Everything, anywhere, everywhere exists all at once. The idea is to use time and space as your tools to discover the things you need to discover and to explore the themes you need to explore in a unique way by forgetting who you are, so you can remember who you are from a different point of view.

### *The One Is the All and the All Are the One*

This, again, simply harkens back to everything existing all at once, and therefore, it is all made out of the same thing. Whether you want to call it God or Goddess or Creator or existence itself doesn't matter. It doesn't mind what you call it because it is everything that is, everyone that is, everywhere that is, and everywhen that is. Nothing else exists but that one thing, and everything is made from it. Everything is a reflection of it and a projection from it.

Imagine yourself standing in the middle of a hall of mirrors. Around you, you see a multitude of infinite reflections from different angles. But in this case, because everything is made out of existence, which is self-aware and consciousness itself, then all of the reflections—those reflections representing all of you, all of us, and every being and thing within existence—are also conscious and self-aware in some way, shape, or form.

It may not be the same form of consciousness or the same expression of consciousness that you consider yourself to be, but nevertheless, everything is made of that consciousness and everything is self-aware in a unique way—even things that don't seem conscious are nonetheless made of it and are a reflection of it.

### *What You Put Out Is What You Get Back*

Some of you call this idea the Law of Attraction. Again, this is universal because everything is a projection of consciousness and a reflection of consciousness. Whatever frequency you operate on, whatever it is you put out in life, is what you get back.

This acts for you as a guiding system. If things are not arranged in a way that you might prefer or if circumstances are not aligned according to your core desires (the truth within you), then you must have a belief system, idea, or definition in contradiction. You then get a reflection back of what frequency you're actually putting out. If you don't like what you're putting out, changing your frequency will allow you to get a reflection back that is more in alignment with what you prefer.

Now, the idea is to use this as a guiding mechanism, understanding your reflections in order to know exactly where you stand, where you are, what you're giving off, and what frequency you're operating from. It's a guiding mechanism to propel you through life and allow you to refine and hone what belief systems to buy into that are more aligned with who you prefer to be and what belief systems to let go of. It is your belief systems that utterly determine what you experience in physical reality. They make up the physical personality. Whatever it is you buy into most strongly is actually what you get back in your experience of physical reality.

### *Everything Changes except the Laws*

The laws are the structure that never changes. They are existence itself and a definition of it. What changes is your experience of that structure, your relationship to it, and your perspective of it. These are what create the expansion of existence: *your experience* of a structure that never changes—your experience that is constantly and infinitely shifting.

Even though the structure is simple and remains the same, described by these five laws, the universe, multiverse, creation, and existence are infinitely expanding through everyone's different perspectives, experiences, and relationships to this simple structure that never changes.

You have the freedom and the free will to decide for yourself what your relationship is to All-That-Is; what your relationship is to existence itself and how you'll experience the expansion of your own individual awareness as the reflection of All-That-Is; and how you'll experience the expansion of the cosmos and the multiverse through your relationship to it in whatever way, shape, or form you decide, for you are given the gift of deciding for yourself, with your self-empowerment and free will, what it is you will experience.

## Your Destiny

You have imposed upon yourselves a kind of destiny in experiencing this theme, this version of you. You are a greater being than this physical, temporary person that you are, but you are part and parcel of a theme you decided upon from a higher level to experience and explore this physical reality. That is your destiny because you've chosen it from the free will of the higher-level spirit, or the Higher Self, that you also are.

You will go through your experience as this personality. That is your so-called destiny. But you have the absolute free will to experience that destiny in any way, shape, or form you wish. If you wish to look at the idea of your theme as a hallway that you've ordered yourself to walk down, to live in and through from beginning to end, well, that's your destiny. But *how* you go down the hallway is up to your free will. You can run; you can fly; you can walk; you can crawl; you can go forwards; you can go backwards; you can be happy or sad. You can look in every doorway along the route, or you can ignore them all and rush to the end in whatever way, shape, or form you so desire. That is how your free will works within the destiny of the theme you have chosen to explore and the personality you have chosen to be for this lifetime.

You have a greater self, of course, that includes the idea of your spirit, soul, oversoul, and higher selves, all the way to All-That-Is. But there's no end to this because you can be different versions of All-That-Is as well. It is infinite in all directions: up, down, in, and out. And therefore, you have the ability, by understanding this simple framework of five laws, to form different relationships with it in whatever way you so desire.

Ponder them until you understand them—*You Exist; Everything Is Here and Now; The One Is the All and the All Are the One; What You Put Out Is What You Get Back; and Everything Changes except the Laws.* Let them be your filtering system when you come across any ideas, especially those that are metaphysical or spiritual. If they don't fit within that framework, if they don't fit with that filter, then what you're dealing with is something that may be a perspective or a belief system that's not necessarily indicative of the actual casual mechanism underlying the spiritual or metaphysical experience you're having.

Use it as your comparative filter system to know the difference between an experiential definition and a mechanical definition of how things actually work. It's all well and good to have an experiential definition. It's just that, many times on your planet, people think that when they have a definition of the experience, they actually have a definition of the mechanism creating that experience, and that isn't always true.

A simplistic example of the difference between these two is to look at the idea you call a sunset. You know that your experience makes it appear as if the sun is actually setting, but you also know now, in this day and age, that that's not actually what's happening. It appears to be setting because your planet is rotating. You're either spinning toward or away from the position of the sun, which makes it appear from your *experience* that the sun is moving through the sky when, in fact, it is your planet that is rotating. The description of the sun setting in no way, shape, or form describes the actual *mechanical* mechanism rotating your planet and creating the experience, the illusion, of a sun setting.

When you start to understand the casual mechanism, it doesn't mean you have to abandon the poetic definition of the experience. You can better understand the actual mechanisms behind it, giving you a clearer understanding of how metaphysical and spiritual experiences are actually created. Then, you don't get lost in the experiential definition, which has existed for thousands of years, that used to keep you from seeing how things actually work: that you create your physical reality with your belief systems.

## The Seven Basic Needs of Physical Life

This leads us to the second part, which we call the Seven Basic Needs of Physical Life. These ideas are being described so that you can understand another difference: the difference between what you often say you want in life and what you actually need in life. Sometimes your wants and your needs coincide; other times, they do not. Specifically, often what you want is not what you need.

What you truly need will fulfill you and allow you to feel fulfilled: to feel joy, to feel an ease of being, and to thrive in physical reality. This is not as true concerning what you want. So, it's important to learn the difference between what you want and what the seven basic needs of physical life actually are.

These will allow you to thrive as a physical being. Without them, you will start to waste away and not be able to perpetuate your physical experience. That's what makes them truly the things you need in order to thrive in physical reality.

We order them based on the severity of your need for each. Again, while this may start out very simplistically, please understand how important they are for you as physical beings having a life on Earth, especially paying close attention to the less expected final points.

*The Seven Basic Needs of Physical Life*

*Your (Usually) Obvious Needs:*

1. Air
2. Water
3. Sleep
4. Food

*Your Less Obvious Needs:*

5. Shelter
6. Connection
7. Creativity

## *Your (Usually) Obvious Needs*

Now, we know there are certain people who practice certain disciplines, such as breatharians, who may seem to get along fine without some of our listed needs for a while, but these are the exceptions. What we're talking about in this list is what the average human does and doesn't need to perpetuate your life.

### *Air*

The first basic need, of course, is air. You need to breathe in order to continue to live. Without breathing, without air, you will probably die within minutes.

### *Water*

You need water. This keeps you fluid and lubricated, literally. You need it to thrive in physical reality. Without it, you will probably die within days.

### *Sleep*

Most people would think that the third thing is food, but it's not. It's actually sleep—dreaming, in particular. If you don't sleep and connect to spirit through your dreams, you'll start hallucinating within ten to eleven days, and your physical systems will start to break down. You'd go psychotic and likely die within two weeks without this connection you usually make each night.

Remember, physical reality isn't what you think it is. It's energy: a projection of consciousness. You are spiritual beings who never leave spirit. You're in spirit right now. All of you exist within spirit. In your "waking hours," you actually dream that you've left spirit to be human. So, right now, as you pretend that you're not spirit, having a physical experience requires—this will change in time—that you "recharge your batteries" to continue projecting the idea that you're a physical being. Your physical lives are illusions; projections that require energy to keep up the illusion that you're just a physical being.

So, you must sleep and dream to keep the physical reality going, to play out your time in space for as long as you've decided to do so.

### *Food*

Number four is food. In some way, shape, or form, most of you on the planet also need sustenance to allow your body to thrive. If you get air, water, sleep, and food, you will begin to thrive.

### *Your Less Obvious Needs*

The concept of needs shifts a little bit in the last three requirements.

### *Shelter*

You all need some form of shelter or environment that is conducive to life. This doesn't mean it has to be a physical house. There are places on your planet, at least for right now, where the environment itself is very pleasurable and very conducive to the thriving of human life. Some people call it tropical islands or refer to it as paradise on Earth, where many people can live outdoors without a shelter or with a very simple shelter to protect them from certain elements.

Normally, however, without shelter or a conducive environment, your body can wear down and you could die. Maybe not right away, but your spirit, in a sense, may also start to diminish when you are feeling stressed out and struggling through life if you're not in an environment that allows your body, spirit, and mind to move forward without having to worry about every little thing, like lightning, floods, earthquakes, and so on.

### *Connection*

Everyone needs connection—a relationship to something or someone. It doesn't even have to be a person. It could be a connection to the cosmos, an animal, the world, a tree, or even a rock. You need a relationship that allows you to feel that you're part of a community or larger group or gives you a communications ability in a relationship with one or many. This idea of belonging is also important for you to thrive in physical reality (as well as other levels of reality).

### *Creativity*

The final need is the creative expression of your true self. In other words, the living of your purpose, your mission, to be you. And that dovetails into the next segment because the idea of expressing the creative essence of your true self—as a giving, serving being—means very specifically one thing: acting on your passions in life, living your dreams, being who you truly know you are in your core, in your heart of hearts, and being willing to act on those things.

These final two (connection and creativity) differ a bit from the first five. Going without either or both doesn't mean you'll die right away, or even quickly at all, but their absence can cause your mind, psychology, and spirit to diminish over time, perhaps even leading to suicidal thoughts, which will take you out of physical reality if you act on them.

## Life's Instruction Manual: The Five-Step Formula

Now, you have the seven basic needs. And if you live or have them, you'll be prepared for fulfilment in every level of your life by simply following the formula we're about to share.

We're about to walk you through the way reality works, describing the actual tools and mechanisms that allow you to create your reality in the way that you prefer—in the way that aligns with who you truly are—to experience the best life possible in the most joyful, creative, passionate, exciting, loving, and connected way possible. *This is not a philosophy.* This is a distillation of the mechanisms through which you actually create your physical reality experience.

We're literally going to give you an instruction manual, in much the same way that you would receive an instruction manual for how to operate a piece of machinery. If you simply follow the basic instructions step-by-step, your "machine" will operate in the way it was designed to, to your advantage. If you don't follow the instructions, well, then the machine may not operate as ideally as it could, and you may, in fact, injure yourself.

This is how you create your physical reality, whether you know it consciously or not. Allow yourself to pay attention and absorb this. We guarantee that if you follow our steps, your life will improve. This is how reality was created and meant to be lived, by you and for you.

*Life's Instruction Manual: The Five-Step Formula*

1. Follow Your Passion
2. Act on Your Passion to the Best of Your Ability
3. Have Zero Insistence on the Outcome
4. Stay in a Positive State
5. Investigate Your Belief Systems

### Follow Your Passion

Again, this section—*Follow Your Passion*—dovetails from the seventh basic need, *Creativity*. Why is this important? You hear this all the time in your reality—follow your bliss, your passion, your excitement. But why? Why is that so important? Allow us to explain.

You have, as a being, a physical mind, but you also have a nonphysical higher mind. And it's your nonphysical higher mind that's meant to guide you through this life. How does it do that? It speaks an energy language. It gives you energetic messages. How do you interpret those energy messages? How do you know when the higher mind is sending you those energy messages? Easy. Your physical body translates those energy messages into the sensations of passion, excitement, creativity, curiosity, attraction, and love. That's how you know you're receiving something from the higher mind: *you feel it in your body*. These feelings tell you that this situation, this circumstance, this thing, this project, this idea, or this concept is something that aligns with who you really are, with your core frequency, experienced as your passion, excitement, creativity, love, and connection. Your frequency is who you are. It's your vibration, your signature as a unique being, a unique reflection of All-That-Is and of existence itself.

### Act on Your Passion to the Best of Your Ability

When you have such feelings about a circumstance, situation, person, or relationship, it's guidance from your higher mind, saying, "This is your next step. This is your path." Act on it the best you can, taking it as far as you can—that's the second step—until you can take it no further. You'll be listening to the higher mind and its guidance—you'll be starting a dialogue with the higher mind and its guidance—and by acting on that passion, you're telling your higher mind, "I heard you. I'm willing to listen. I'm open to it and to receiving your guidance because you are guiding me through life in the best possible way."

The language of the higher mind in *physical reality* isn't words; it's actions. So, when you act, you're speaking back, saying, "Yes, I heard you, and I'm willing to act on this passion because you're telling me that this is who I am right now." Then, continue onward, acting on your passion for as long as you can, taking it as far as you can, until you can take it no further or until your excitement wanes.

There are two reasons why your excitement or passion may temporarily or permanently wane in the direction of the thing you're acting on:

1. It's an opportunity to examine your belief systems to ensure there isn't a fear-based or negative belief causing the excitement to go away, perhaps because you're too afraid to move forward or you're worried that something bad will happen if you do.
2. If it's naturally going away, then it's synchronicity telling you to change course: that your next step may be something you haven't thought of yet, to look for something else that contains more excitement than anything else, and to move on *that* next, act on *that* next. Most paths are not necessarily straight lines. Yours may be a winding path that will actually be the shortest of all because it's the path of least resistance.

We'll talk more about synchronicities shortly. For right now, the idea is to act on your passion, taking it as far as you can until you can take it no further, while ensuring you're not the one lessening it because you have fear-based beliefs about what it means to move forward.

### Have Zero Insistence on the Outcome

Then, the next part—and I understand that this is a great challenge for many—as you act on your passion, taking it as far as you can, *you must have absolutely zero, and I mean zero, insistence or assumption on what the outcome should be or for what it will look like.*

The key to this is understanding that your physical mind is limited in its capacity to imagine what the *ideal* outcome actually is. Yet you all have powerful imaginations, and you can and should use them, while dropping your insistence on outcomes. This is much easier than it may first seem.

Visualization is not necessarily a tool for the purpose of manifesting *exactly* what you imagine, although sometimes this happens. It's meant to create a representation or to serve as a kind of placeholder for the truly ideal outcome. What you imagine is to be a symbol for the purpose of getting you into the excitement you need to be in to actually give and receive guidance from the higher mind. It is to be emblematic of what the real outcome needs to be or what the next thing is that needs to happen that's good for your journey and positive for your path.

So, by dropping your idea of the outcome after you've used it to get really excited about the manifestation, that's when you open up. By staying excited, you create space for the higher mind to deliver what needs to happen next—what will serve you best. Then, no matter what shows up, stay in a positive state to keep the momentum going. That's the trick. That's the key.

### *Stay in a Positive State*

Even if something manifests that you don't prefer—objectively speaking, not a judgment—recognize that whatever it is, *it will still serve you if you stay in a positive state.*

Sometimes, when you get really good at this, you'll even test yourself by manifesting something you don't prefer, to see if you're going to react to it negatively in the same old way you used to. The true measure of change is not whether the outside world looks different; it's whether you respond to it differently, even when it looks the same. If you truly understand these principles, it wouldn't matter to you what happens next because you know it will serve you, even if it was created from a negative place.

This doesn't mean that you'll start calling a negative thing a positive thing unto itself. What it means is you can recognize that even though something may have been created out of negative energy, you can still get a positive result from it if you remain in a positive energetic state. Remember, you can only experience what you are the vibration of. What you put out is what you get back. That's the law. It's just plain physics.

The idea, then, is that by staying in a positive state, even when something manifests that you don't prefer, you'll be able to use it in a positive way. For example, seeing something that you *don't* prefer can give you a much clearer idea, by contrast and comparison, of what you *do* prefer, which is a positive way to use what you don't prefer. And as soon as you use it that way, it will disappear and the things that you do prefer can start coming in.

Here's the big secret about the Law of Attraction: there's a misunderstanding that says you have to learn to create the frequency you're after.

No. Those frequencies of passion, excitement, creativity, love, and connection are your natural state. These are your core vibrations, remember? They are designed to attract absolutely everything relevant in your life that will permit you to experience those qualities at all times.

You're always sending out those vibrations. They're always attempting to attract everything you prefer and that you need for your own fulfilment. You don't have to learn to create those frequencies. It's about getting out of your own way, letting go of fear-based and negative beliefs that are interfering with your natural frequencies and your innate ability to attract what you need into your life.

### *Investigate Your Belief Systems*

Focus on the idea of understanding your belief systems. Investigate your belief systems, finding the ones that don't work for you, are out of date, out of alignment, or probably belonged to someone else. Growing up in life, you absorbed the beliefs of those who cared for you—your parents, friends, school, society—telepathically and through body language, beliefs that simply had nothing to do with you or that sprung from their own unfulfilled wishes.

But now that you've grown up, you can think for yourself. You can decide what's true for you. You can let go of the belief systems you may have gathered along the way that are out of alignment with your core vibration to allow your core frequencies to work in the most efficient way.

### *Using Life's Instruction Manual*

The main ideas of the instruction manual or formula are to act on your passion every moment that you can, to the best of your ability, to take it as far as you can until you can go no further, making sure you're not dampening the excitement with fear-based beliefs, and then look for the next thing that contains more excitement than any other option and act on that next. That's your path, and that's what your higher mind is telling you.

Do this without any insistence or assumption on what the outcome should look like or be, when it should happen, or how it should happen. Open to the idea that your higher mind and synchronicity will bring you what's most ideal: your absolute best outcome. And then, allow yourself to stay positive, no matter what manifests, so you can benefit from it and extract a positive experience. Even if a thing that manifests is something you don't prefer, use it in a positive way.

Along the way, examine your belief systems. Investigate the ideas you're buying into as true for yourself in any given situation with honesty and willingness. Ask, "Why do I believe something bad may happen? Why have I picked up on a particular fear that something might go wrong?" Allow yourself to examine why it's there, what it is, and let it go by making it nonsensical. See your negative beliefs in a true and fair light. Compare yourself to other people in the world who might be doing things you would love to do. See them as representatives of what your own passion is capable of.

When you can see others thriving, it's clearly an indication that you can too, at least in some way, shape, or form, if not identically to them. And see how the fact that they can do it and somehow it seems you can't is nonsensical. Understand that if it really was true that you couldn't do it, you would never even be able to see other people doing it!

Now, that doesn't mean everyone can do every single thing that other people are doing. The idea is to be honest with yourself about what your dreams and passions truly are and what is relevant for you in your life. Relevance is the key here. "Could I suddenly become a blue being that is twelve feet tall with fifteen arms?" Well, it is possible. But is it probable? Is it relevant? Not likely, given your path, your theme, and what you're exploring.

It's not about what's possible or impossible. It's about what's probable or relevant for you. Be honest with yourself about what you truly need in life to be fulfilled by following what we have shared with you so far, and you will find that your life can be very simple (relatively speaking), you can gain the things you need very simply, and you can be absolutely ecstatic with the way it all unfolds.

To repeat once again, act on your passion. Take it as far as you can. Allow yourself to determine why any enthusiasm has waned. Be honest with yourself. Stay in a positive state. Don't insist or assume what the outcome should be. Examine your belief systems so that you can let go of the ones that are no longer relevant—that are negative and fear based. And be true to yourself about what's possible in your life.

There are no more instructions. We could spend hours, and we have—in fact, we've spent years—going into the details of precisely how these instructions need to be applied in your reality. Precision is the key here. You cannot add other ideas or outdated belief systems to this formula and expect the formula to work as precisely as it can.

We have given you the stripped-down version of the mechanisms you already use to create your physical reality experience. We give it to you in the simplest possible way so that it doesn't become overly complicated and so you don't have to overthink it. You can just apply it purely and simply for whatever you deem correct for you. It will change your life, guaranteed, if you apply it properly.

## Finding Your Passion

We know that in our conversations with many of you, you say, "Well, I don't know what my passion is." Nonsense. It's easy to find your passion. But when we say passion, we are not trying to conjure up images of some life-spanning career or some gigantic project. No. We mean to simply start something.

You have the ability to determine which options before you are more exciting, for which you have more passion, attraction, or even curiosity, than the other options in your life, even if it's just a little bit more than the other options. So, start simply. If you don't have a big idea of what that means, start small. It will snowball into something bigger.

For example, you are reading this book—we assume—because you thought this was the most exciting thing you could be doing in this particular moment. That wasn't hard to do. It wasn't a difficult decision. You just said, "Oh, yes, out of all the options I have, I'm going to do this because I'm more attracted to it right now."

Once your reading is all over, look around. You could take a walk, read a different book, see a movie, talk to a friend, eat a meal, have a nap, whatever. By comparing your options, if any of them has even the tiniest bit more attractiveness or passion or excitement in it than any other option, simply do it next, to the best of your ability, following the formula. *You never know where that's going to lead, and that's the whole point.*

It will always lead you to the next place you actually need to be—even if it seems totally disconnected—in ways you simply cannot comprehend. Let's say you're writing a book, and for some reason you feel you just can't go any further. The excitement has waned. The ideas aren't coming. You look around and think, "All right, well, what's the next most exciting thing I could do? Hmmm...I'd like to take a walk." So, you take a walk. And while walking, you happen to overhear a conversation that is exactly what you needed to inspire you for the next chapter of your book.

*That's how it works when you let it.* That's pure synchronicity—and that is the organizing principle of your life. It is one of the mechanisms that unfolds when you follow the formula.

## Synchronicity

Now, the final part of our review will look more closely at this mechanism and how it unfolds when you precisely apply our Life's Instruction Manual and its five steps as diligently and often as possible.

Synchronicity is always working. Everything's an orchestration. In truth, there are no accidents. You are always where you are through perfect synchronicity, and whether that's a positive or a negative synchronicity is up to you and your state of being. By negative synchronicity, we mean that if you are in a negative state, buying into negative, fear-based beliefs, this will allow you to spiral downward, causing more and more negative circumstances to surround you.

But there are two forms of positive synchronicity, what we refer to as red light synchronicity and green light synchronicity, that arise. For example, when an opportunity representative of your passion may present itself to you so that you are able to act on it.

Sometimes, there's something that looks like an opportunity, but when you do your best to act on it you don't get anywhere. It's like banging into a brick wall. Now, unless this is caused by a negative belief system, it might be red light synchronicity simply saying, "Not right now." This may be representative of your path or representative of your passion, but this red light means it's not the next step to take right now.

In which case, if you've examined yourself and you believe wholeheartedly and honestly that it is not a fear-based belief that's preventing you from moving down that path, but positive synchronicity in the red-light sense that is saying not right now, then look for other things you can act on and move in that direction. That's your guiding mechanism again.

These unexpected diversions actually increase the acceleration of your journey, finding your path of least resistance. There doesn't need to be struggle in your life. You don't need to exert that much effort. Yes, there are still challenges, but challenges are fun. There's no need to define them in a negative way.

When you're following your passion, these accelerations add to the driving engine of your life and give you the energy to keep going. They move and motivate you. You can't wait to get up in the morning and keep going. This is what happens when you follow the formula of acting on your passion to the best you can, no insistence or assumption on the outcome, while you stay in a positive state no matter what happens, examining and letting go of your negative and fear-based beliefs.

The organizing principle of synchronicity brings you exactly what you need to act on, when you need to act on it, in perfect timing. If it's not coming to you right now, it doesn't need to. Trust the way your life unfolds. Synchronicity will guide you.

Any strain and negativity cease to be felt. You're flowing through life. You're following your unique current, a current that connects you to all other expressions of your excitement so that when red light synchronicity says, "No, not this," green light synchronicity says, "Over here, look at this; this is the next step for you to take."

It also connects you to all the forms of support you need in your life for you to continue to act on your excitement. And when I say support, I don't just mean money. I understand that money is one of the symbols of abundance and support in your reality, on your planet, but it isn't the only one. When you insist that it *has* to be money or else you can't do what you need to do, you're actually closing the door *to all the other forms of abundance* that could allow you to move forward on your passion, your excitement, and your dream.

## Abundance and Support for the Journey

Money is valid but it isn't always necessary, and you may not need as much of it as you think to move forward in your life. Being given a gift is also a form of abundance. Having something to trade is a form of abundance. Synchronicity itself is a form of abundance. Imagination is a form of abundance, because it may allow you to conjure up some idea or some concept that you didn't think of before. Communication is a form of abundance, because when you start communicating to the people in your life about where you're at and what's going on and what your dreams are all about, you may find an incredible amount of support in ways you never imagined before.

Remain open to receive all forms of abundance as you act and move forward so that it can arrive in many ways until you have all you need. Maybe some money will show up, maybe somebody will give you a gift, maybe somebody will share an idea with you, maybe you'll have something to trade; then, altogether, what you receive will cover one hundred percent of the abundance you needed to move forward in your joy and your passion.

Don't close the doors to all the other forms of abundance by insisting—remember, no assumptions, no insistence—on the fact that you think you need this kind of money or that kind of money in order to follow your passion. Let the doors open, and let the abundance and synchronicity show you what you need. Don't assume that you know what that is. Don't insist that you know. Insistence is resistance to the natural flow of things in your life.

When you leave the doors open, all things that are then relevant in your life will come to you. The things that are not relevant won't. Trust and allow the way your life unfolds. Trust the timing of when things show up. Don't push. Don't resist.

## The Reflective Mirror

The final tool, the final step in following this formula—examining your belief system—is what we also call the *reflective mirror*. As you act on your excitement and your passion, the reflective mirror will constantly bring up anything in your belief system that is not in alignment with your passion so you can deal with it, find out why it's there, and let it go. Adding renewed energy to your momentum, excitement, and passion.

Should you be flowing in your excitement when, suddenly, some old negative fear-based belief crops up, realize this is not an obstacle, just an interruption. It's part of your path to discover an inner contradiction within your unconscious mind so that you can deal with it, let it go, and add that energy to your excitement. This way, finding things within your belief system that don't excite you becomes part of your excitement. It's all about staying positive no matter what comes up.

When you stay in a positive state, examine your belief systems, and let go of the negative and fear-based ones, your life suddenly goes on automatic pilot. Yes, there are challenges, but now they're fun because you have the right attitude, the right energy, and the right state of being. This is what determines the quality of your life, not your circumstances. It's your state of being in those circumstances. It's how you respond to what happens, not what happens, that makes the difference.

Life itself suddenly becomes the driving engine of your journeys, your dance with synchronicity. You're motivated. You're constantly excited to act on those things. Everything starts showing up at the right time, in the right order. What you didn't do on any given day didn't need to be done that day. Synchronicity allows you to experience the path of least resistance. It allows you to experience the path of connection to all other forms and expressions of your excitement. It forges your path of relevance.

Your life will guide you to what is truly relevant for you. It allows you to experience the idea of support in all its forms—to keep going, acting on your excitement. Simply remain open to all the forms in which abundance and support can come; don't shut them down by insisting that only one thing will work in your life, or you'll never know how else it could have appeared. Your reflective mirror will then bring to your conscious attention any belief systems within you that are out of alignment with who you are.

That's what fear is: a messenger. You have just one energy, and it's always one hundred percent on. But it filters through your belief systems that create your personality. What you believe in is who you are. When you filter your energy through positive belief systems that are in alignment with your core vibrations, you won't be afraid of anything. You'll move forward knowing that everything can serve you and that you can serve everything in a positive way.

If you have negative or fear-based belief systems, then you're filtering your energy through those. You will feel fear. And consider: negative belief systems have to perpetuate themselves just like positive ones, or you wouldn't have a physical reality to experience. Remember, physical reality is an illusion. *There is no physical reality other than your perceptions of it. Your perceptions are your reality.* The way it maintains its apparent solidity is through you buying into something you believe to be true about you in relation to any given situation within the physical reality experience.

When you buy into positive beliefs about yourself in a situation, that's not usually a "problem" because you're happy. But when you buy into negative beliefs about yourself in a situation, you look at yourself judgmentally and negatively, and you think, "I'm not worthy. I'm not capable. I'm no good. I have nothing to offer. I'm this. I'm that." These beliefs, these perceptions, become your truth. Then, these ideas reinforce themselves, because all beliefs have to perpetuate themselves in some way, shape, or form in order for you to continue to have a physical reality experience.

Accordingly, negative beliefs will use every mechanism available to prevent you from letting them go. That's just the way it works. It's not a malicious thing. It's not an intentional thing. It's just the way beliefs are designed to allow you to continue to experience physical reality. Negative beliefs will make you afraid to let them go, prevent you from letting them go, and thereby, prevent you from moving forward on your passion.

You have to see this as simply the way beliefs work and not take it personally, struggle with it, or be afraid of it. Fear lets you know. Fear is your friend. It's a messenger telling you something is being misunderstood. When you feel it, afraid to move forward on your passion, your fear is saying, "Hey, hey, I'm letting you know you're feeling me because you're filtering your energy through a negative belief system." If you don't prefer that, find out what you believe and why. How does holding on to it serve you? Because you only hold on to things you believe serve you in some way, shape, or form.

It works without fail. You will always, no exceptions, move toward what you believe serves you. And you will always move away from what you believe does not serve you. So, moving away from something you want should be your first clue that you have a belief somewhere, conscious or unconscious, urging you to choose an option that doesn't serve you.

You have to switch that in your motivational mechanism and ask, "Why would I believe that this thing will turn out badly? That it may not turn out as I first expected, which I already know will serve me if I stay in a positive state, as I have just learned? No matter what happens, I will absolutely be able to use it to my advantage. So, what difference will it make what actually happens? What difference does it make if it doesn't come out as I expected? It makes no difference at all, because I am self-empowered as a cocreator with All-That-Is to determine what meaning it will have in my life, why it's there, and how I can use it to create my reality of preference."

That's your gift: the power to choose. It's the greatest gift you've been given. You are a cocreator. Choose the meaning. Life in a sense—don't take this negatively—is meaningless. It has no built-in meaning. *You* are designed to give it meaning. The meaning you decide to give it is the effect you'll get out of it. That's your greatest power.

So, choose between your belief systems, choose the meaning you're putting into things, and choose the definitions you've been taught that may crop up automatically. Examine your beliefs. Ask, "Why do I believe something is true?" Find out where that comes from. Let it go if it doesn't work for you.

Most people have very little idea of their powers in this way, and that's their option. It's also an option for you.

## Putting It All Together

This is The Self-Realization Tool Kit. It's what will allow your vibration to rise constantly and allow you to ascend into a higher version of physical reality, as well as beyond, into a nonphysical reality where you will still have an infinite array of choices to consider and experience. It never ends. There's no such thing as a beginning or an ending to existence itself. Remember, those are concepts within existence. Existence just is. That's its only quality. Just to be, to be, to be. Time and space are creations within existence. Existence is not subject to time and space. It's infinite; it's eternal. You'll always have somewhere new to experience and something new to explore, and that's exciting.

So, find that passion at any level and act on it to the best of your ability. It will serve you and allow you to serve others by being a living example of how to live a fulfilled life on Earth and how to create Heaven on Earth—not that they have to choose it. Remember, everyone has their own path. You'll be showing people a different way they could be doing things that might be more beneficial to them, but what they do with that information is none of your business, just as what you do with the information I'm sharing is none of my business. You have your own path. I am giving you what works. But it's up to you to decide what processes you use. It's really *your* path.

Share with others when it's appropriate to do so. You've done all you can by simply making it an option for them. Who knows? Maybe they'll choose it in ten years, in twenty years, or in another lifetime. It doesn't matter. You're eternal. What's the hurry?

---

*That was crystal clear and very doable. Thank you, Bashar. To confirm, our passions come from our Higher Selves?*

---

Yes.

---

*Are there ever needs beyond the clear seven that you gave? For example, might I need to increase my self-confidence? Or to eliminate fear? And does need enter the equation of sorting our passions?*

Yes. This is why we tell you in that instruction manual there is the reflective mirror that brings to your attention any beliefs that are out of alignment with who you truly are so that you have the opportunity to clear them out. That's why we're saying this is a complete kit. It contains everything relevant you need in life. There is nothing extra that's required. It has all the elements necessary to bring you every single concept and awareness necessary to go through life as the perfect being that you are at your core.

*You talked about beliefs being the ultimate barrier in our lives. You also talked about us being here, focused within the density of time and space. Is our presence here anchored by the belief that we are here or is ego involved? Is there a difference between the anchor of the ego and beliefs?*

You made a choice in spirit to have a physical experience, speaking linearly (I have to use a timeframe so you'll understand more clearly).

To have a physical experience as spiritual beings, you must impose a kind of filtering system on part of your consciousness to eliminate, or phase out from your focus, things that are broader than the definition of the physical experience. You do this by creating belief systems, which result in a personality, or an ego structure, that will keep you focused within your life. An ego is simply the focus of a personality for experiencing the idea of physicality.

This is similar, by analogy, to an underwater diving mask. If you go diving in the ocean, it's easier for you to see where you're going if you wear a diving mask that makes things clear. Otherwise, it can be a little fuzzy or a little murky. The diving mask is analogous to the physical ego: ego allows you to experience clarity, while making physical reality seem real to you so that ego can function within physical reality. But the diving mask doesn't tell you where you should go. It just shows you what you're seeing more clearly.

When people give the ego structure more to do than it's designed for, it can take on negative qualities, thinking it's in control or that it needs to control everything. It feels like it needs to know everything before it happens instead of just showing you clearly what is happening in the moment so that you can live with it or deal with it in the way you prefer.

The idea is to let the ego do its simple job of being clear about where you are, not to allow it to think that it actually knows what's going to happen. That's the purview of the higher mind. And that's why the higher mind brings you those messages through the form of excitement and passion, to guide you through life unerringly when you pay attention to those feelings. Does that help?

*That helps a great deal. So, the ego is more than a confluence of our beliefs? It's our mask or a filter that helps us see clearly, and then we work with our beliefs?*

Again, the belief creates what appears to be the dependability and continuity of your reality. In other words, beliefs use emotion, thoughts, and behaviors to reinforce themselves and make themselves seem factual.

Physical reality isn't a fact; it isn't real. It's a projection. Beliefs reinforce themselves, positive and negative, using emotion to make it feel real, using thoughts to make you think it's real, and using behaviors to make you act like it's real, all of which creates the reflection of your experiences. Your entire reality is the product of your emotions, thoughts, and behaviors, all the way back to the belief system.

Beliefs form the blueprint of what you are experiencing. Your emotions—emotion derived from energy and motion—are the builders. Your thought patterns are, in a sense, the materials you're building with. Your behaviors are the way you go about building things with those materials (i.e., your thoughts).

For this metaphor, your experience is the house you've built based on the blueprint of the beliefs you started with. Whenever something is off-kilter in the house—the reality that you're experiencing—go back through the behaviors, the thoughts, and the emotions, and realize that none of those can exist without first having the blueprint—the belief. By working backwards like this, you can ultimately discover which of your beliefs aren't serving you.

Emotions can't exist in a vacuum. You have to believe that something is true before you can feel that it's real. Beliefs use your emotions to reinforce themselves in order to make physical reality seem like a fact—touchable, tangible, and real. But when you begin to understand your experiences exist because of what you believe to be true about yourself, well, then you can always go back to the belief and adjust it or find a new one that serves you better, which will then change the emotions, the thoughts, the behaviors, and the experiences up the line.

*To confirm, following your tool kit by taking steps aligned with our passions, we will be led to "out" our hang-ups, so to speak, so we can ultimately pare them down to little or none, which is often called self-realization.*

Yes. And the idea is, even once you have let go of all the negative or fear-based beliefs, you can still continue in life to simply let go of all the things that are no longer relevant for you as a living being.

*Is this the cusp that we are on now, planetarily and/or individually? Are we approaching that line of full self-realization?*

You're not approaching it; *you're in the middle of it.* This is a time of profound change, presenting the opportunity for you each to shift your lives in the direction of creating the reality and the version of Earth that you prefer. There are multiple parallel reality versions of Earth that simultaneously coexist, and whatever vibrational frequency you navigate yourself toward will be the version of Earth that you wind up on. All the other versions will still exist. Those who choose a negative path will wind up on the negative versions. Those who choose a more positive path will wind up on a positive version. All these versions exist right now.

It's a matter of navigating the path you're on right now: the way you shift—because you're constantly shifting. But it's about the quality. It's about the vibrational frequency. It's about the resonance that you operate on that determines where you ultimately wind up.

This is the split, the splitting prism, that you're in the middle of right now that will determine what you'll ultimately experience in the years to come. Right now, you can see each other's realities. You can see the choices everyone is making. But just because you can see them doesn't mean you're heading into the same reality. It's like looking at another reality through a glass wall. They can't reach you. You can see them, but they can't affect you and you can't affect them unless they choose to be affected.

The idea is to use this time to make choices about what kind of a reality you prefer, act in the manner that demonstrates what kind of a reality you prefer, and be of service as a living example to let everyone know there are different options to choose from. In the years to come, those options will fade away, and you will only experience people that are of a like-mind to you, whether positive or negative, on your version of Earth. Right now, you have the opportunity to examine all the different possibilities and choose the ones that work for you.

---

*Would it be fair to say that, in the imminent future, we may reach a tipping point where the collective breaks through and knows the true nature of reality—that all things are possible—and all follow their passion, in touch with their Higher Selves? Is this happening right now? Is there a point when we'll know that we made it past this tipping point?*

It may take a little while. But the point is you're not changing the planet you're on. You're leaving the planet you're on and going to a different version of Earth that is already that way and already populated with the versions of yourselves that are in alignment with the frequency that you're talking about. You never change the world you're on; you change yourself and take yourself to a different Earth that is more reflective of the change you made within.

You will experience this transformation upon a linear timeline, just as you experience your life today. It will seem as if the world has changed, but it won't be the original world. You're shifting billions of times a second right now, literally. You're never on the same planet. Millions of times per second you're never the same person. This is what creates the illusion of time, change, and motion. This a different reality. This is a different reality. This is a different reality. This is a different reality. This is a different reality. Literally, each are totally different.

When you wrap your minds around the fact that every moment is a "zero," that you define in the moment with the themes you've agreed to experience and the processes you've agreed to go through, you will then realize that you are cleaned billions of times a second, as you choose what you prefer to experience by simply changing your thoughts.

That's why we want you to understand how things work; then you can use this information to your advantage more consciously. It's not about having to *learn* to do something new. It's about learning that you're already doing it and then just choosing to do it in a way that you prefer, instead of a way that you don't.

---

*"Bashar, can you explain the reason that a higher dimensional being chooses to become a lower dimensional being?"*

---

It's the same reason on a different scale that you as a physical human might want to experience the thrill of watching a scary movie. It teaches you different things. It's a different experience. It puts you in touch with different aspects of yourself. Why not? If you know that anything and everything can be used to your advantage, then nothing is off limits. So, why not?

---

*"In other teachings of yours, you often make reference to our use of 'permission slips.' Can you briefly explain the concept of 'permission slips'?"*

---

Permission slips are those rites, rituals, and practices that (you think) grant you permission to believe as you wish to believe, usually to elevate yourself, ascend, and raise your frequency. These practices could be prayer, meditation, or foods you eat. It doesn't matter what it is. If it's in your belief system, then it is something that will work for you. It could also be the idea of reading tea leaves. It could be the idea of tarot cards. It could be vision boards, affirmations, or crystal balls. It could be any prosaic physical thing or gesture in your reality that you deem necessary in order to become more of who you are.

Of course, you're the one making the change. It's just that you're imbuing certain objects and activities with the power to change you when, in fact, you're changing yourself. Ultimately, you realize that the permission slip is just a symbol. You've been the one changing yourself all along. And ultimately, you become your own permission slip to change in whatever way, shape, or form you prefer, without needing a symbol to do that.

*Are we on the verge of being able to raise our vibration so high that we can teleport, shapeshift, and ascend?*

There are a few people on your planet who are now capable of doing that—a few. Not many of you have reached that level and not many of you need to at this point. Don't assume or insist that being able to do those things is the ultimate expression of physical reality. There are many expressions of physical reality that are just as valid and just as spiritual. Someone who simply retains what appears to be a relatively normal physical life can be even more spiritual than people who have learned to do those things. It just depends on how you're using it.

*"Gene Roddenberry [screenwriter and producer who created the science fiction franchise* Star Trek*] is said to have attended channelings of a Council of Nine, which influenced the* Star Trek *series. How should we evaluate the authenticity of* Star Trek*–portrayed realities?"*

Again, many of them may be representative to some degree of a parallel existence and may have a percentage of accuracy in that. You can't necessarily assume that all of them are one hundred percent representative of different parallel realities, at least in the physical sense.

Anything is possible in the nonphysical world, and those kinds of scenarios can be recreated in spirit to any degree you desire.

There are many creative people, such as writers of television series, who have either consciously or unconsciously tapped into what's going on in the outer cosmos. For example, Gene Coon came up with the idea of the Prime Directive, which holds that extraterrestrial life should maintain a hands-off approach concerning worlds that don't yet understand the existence of other civilizations in the cosmos.

This is an example of someone in a creative state tapping into something that's actually true out here among extraterrestrial beings who are dealing with Earth and other planets. We only share, shall we say, a limited amount of understanding until you develop and evolve to a point where you can handle more of what we're all about. We want you to decide for yourselves what path you will take. We will not intervene beyond a certain point, in order to give you an understanding of your own power and your own free will.

---

*Are you physically watching and aware of this transmission through Darryl right now, somewhere on a spaceship or elsewhere?*

---

My scout ship is above your area called Sedona, Arizona, twelve hundred miles above Bell Rock, right now. So, yes, I am monitoring this through the channel and in a variety of other physical ways.

---

*Thank you so much, Bashar and Darryl, though "thank you" seems hardly enough.*

---

It's our passion and pleasure to interact with each and every one of you. We give you all our unconditional support and love. You're each beautiful spiritual beings. Know that, act like it, and your world and your lives will be transformed.

We bid you an exciting day of discovery and play. Good day. And in my own ancient language, "A'veyo," which means, "I'm in service to you."

---

*To find out more about Darryl, his books, and Bashar, please visit www.darrylanka.com or www.bashar.org.*

# Epilogue

In June 2021, a year before hosting the online course that would become the genesis of this book, with my interest in self-realization and embodied enlightenment soaring, I reached out to Tracy Farquhar, my friend and co-author of *Channeled Messages from Deep Space: Wisdom for a Changing World*. I invited Frank, a collective she channels from a planet they call Brohashka, to shed some light on the nature of self-realization and to speak on whether or not it's the ultimate goal of our human existence.

While the wisdom of their tempered reply was not fully evident to me at the time, as I've grown so has my deep appreciation for it. Profound, on point, even cautionary, it synchronistically makes the perfect epilogue for, and confirmation of, the preceding pages, with intriguing insights into the lives of known masters who've graced the face of Earth.

## Enlightenment versus Transcendence

In order to fully understand any concept such as enlightenment, one must detach from the preconceived notions and theories surrounding it, since those notions and theories are constructs of the human mind, which, while fully realized as miraculous, have limitations in their ability to understand the workings of consciousness and spirit.

Even now, you are working within the limitations of the human mind, except when you cease trying intellectually to understand and begin spiritually to embrace the nature of yourself as an unlimited being. Your nature is an energetic one, and it is presently expressing itself as a physical form. That physical form creates limitations, some of which may be overcome and some which cannot, for that is the intention of incarnating in the physical state.

Enlightenment is a transcendent state, and while many humans and other beings have reached an advanced state of energetic frequency congruent with your limited ideas of enlightenment, to be *fully* transcended from their experience is not the goal of the human or any physical experience. If it were, what would be the point except to test the limitations of a "lesser" physical experience? Would that not negate the sacredness of that experience?

The goal or intention of a physical being is to provide the soul with a unique perspective that is unavailable any other way and, through that experience, to fulfill the soul's curiosity and desire to expand its consciousness, continually, without having an end point of complete transcendence.

Nevertheless, aspiring to live in a state which brings light, which emanates light, which encourages light, is inherent in all consciousness, both to minimize suffering and to experience greater joy. That light contains truth, compassion, acceptance, and high states of both spiritual and physical awareness, for you are both.

And while some have dedicated their lives to living with greater illumination, their experience will simply become one of many in the energetic intelligence of their soul, no more and no less important than any other. The masters who walked your Earth were human, in every way, and while they imparted an elevated sense of wisdom and truth, they did not transcend the human experience. Their intention was to assist and support those who struggle and suffer, and to impart the truth of love as a balm for the wounded and the unloved. It was to inspire and create a flow of loving energy. To us, that is the highest degree of enlightenment that a human or any other form of incarnated physical being can experience.

We will not deign to understand all there is to understand about the reasons and object of the soul's decision to incarnate physically. But as we have become a bit more educated in the realm of consciousness, we see the sacredness of every level of energetic frequency and every form of physical incarnation and every step upon the path that each individual takes as it walks in that physical form. It is all sacred, it is all transcendent, and it is all a form of enlightenment.

We also believe that the more you strive for something, the more it slips through your fingers as that striving interrupts the flow of your frequency and distracts you from the present moment. Cease striving, and you will achieve. Cease wanting to understand, and you will allow that understanding to flow through you. Cease wanting to be more aware, and that awareness will blossom. Be that light that you seek, and within that light, you will have the highest experience of what this lifetime has to offer you.

*—Frank, channeled by Tracy Farquhar, www.tracyfarquhar.com*

*"You can 'come awake' from your normal waking state, and that is the natural next step for consciousness to follow—one for which your biology has already equipped you."*

—Jane Roberts, *The Individual and the Nature of Mass Events*

# Recommended Reading

Here are the books that helped pave my way (*and totally lit me up*) for the creation of *The Great Awakening*.

***The Starseed Trilogy* by Ken Carey**
*The Starseed Transmissions*, *The Third Millennium*, and *Return of the Bird Tribes* predict an entirely new world order in the millennium we're now beginning to be filled with fully self-realized spiritual leaders. Absolutely riveting, empowering, instructional, and often poetic, with some of the most original ideas I've ever read.

***Conversations with God, Book 4: Awaken the Species***
**by Neale Donald Walsch**
As the title suggests, this book is all about awakening. Told from the same lofty perspective as the first three books in this extremely compelling series, this book is filled with perspectives of how Highly Evolved Beings (HEBs) choose to live their lives and organize their worlds based upon love and a recognition that all are one, one is all, and everything is God.

***The Nature of Personal Reality (A Seth Book)* by Jane Roberts**
Like all her Seth books, this one is deep, objective, and a bit complex. This series is more about understanding and fully living one's life, supported by extraordinary views on reality, rather than raising one's vibration to achieve embodied self-realization, although through such a mastery, your vibrations will nevertheless soar.

***The Hermetica: The Lost Wisdom of the Pharaohs***
**by Timothy Freke and Peter Gandy**
Summarizes some of the scattered and legendary teachings of the Greek god Hermes and the mythical Egyptian sage Thoth. Their

writings are part of a fabled work otherwise known as *The Emerald Tablets*. An absolutely stunning and mind-binding read, both the translations (from ancient Greek) and the authors' commentary. I especially enjoyed reading Thoth's description of what it feels like to suddenly be made one with Atum (God) in a moment of illumination.

***Ramtha (The White Book)* by Ramtha**
Very friendly, powerful, and inspirational. An easy read, yet one of the most powerful of all the titles listed here.

***The Golden Lake: Wisdom from the Stars for Life on Earth* by Lyssa Royal Holt**
Profound insights from the Pleiades into soul-integration, the evolution of consciousness, and how one awakens to the higher realms of spirit. It includes excellent exercises, analogies, and metaphors for easier understanding.

***The Prism of Lyra: An Exploration of Human Galactic Heritage* by Lyssa Royal Holt**
Best explanation *ever* (deep and expansive) of ETs, their origins, and what they've been up to.

***The Untethered Soul* and *The Surrender Experiment* by Michael A. Singer**
The author is a modern-day pioneer into consciousness, who believes that *life itself* is the ultimate spiritual path. The author's insights in both of these books are truly astounding, especially as they relate to getting out of one's own head, where we tend to overthink everything, making enlightenment otherwise "impossible."

***Siddhartha* by Hermann Hesse**
Profound and exciting wisdom in a timeless, world-famous novel. It culminates with the awakening of the story's hero, sharing exquisite detail of his revelations and transcendence of ego.

***Autobiography of a Yogi* by Paramahansa Yogananda**
This is an account of spiritual seeking and finding. It portrays full enlightenment as possible for every human and views it as a worthy "goal." It contains many accounts of exciting supernatural encounters and paranormal events.

***Bringers of the Dawn: Teachings from the Pleiadians***
**by Barbara Marciniak**
While there are small portions of this book I either do not understand or disagree with (such as some ETs trying to influence humans for their own gain), this gem is extremely eye-opening. It frequently speaks of a human potential that we can achieve through self-realization that parallels the Ken Carey books recommended above.

***The Convoluted Universe* by Dolores Cannon**
A *fascinating* series filled with mind-bending ideas of our origins and the potential of spirit. Dolores can be found on YouTube saying, "Everything is energy. And you come to Earth to learn how to manipulate it. To be a master manifester."

***Two Crystals from Lemuria* by Margaret L. Brandeis**
An exciting, very short read. You will never look at crystals in the same way again, and what these crystals share about ascension took my breath away.

***Ascension* by Daniel Scranton**
Another great series that will inspire you to go within. The author also has a fabulous and free daily channeled email, one of the very few I faithfully read.

# Acknowledgements

I'm deeply grateful to the team behind-the-scenes at tut.com that helped bring this book, and all else I do, to life. Hope Koppelman, your warmth, creativity, and passion for excellence sets the bar high for us all. Ivy Guiler, your marketing and technology savoir faire have raised our game countless levels. Regena Garrepy, your team building and leadership skills have put our trainers on virtually every continent. Gina Tyquiengco, your eye for design, coding, and all things beautiful makes us look amazing. Karli Smith, your tenacity under pressure and clarity amidst chaos inspire us. Jolie Woodstock Jackson, your accounting prowess means our footing is always on solid ground, even when our heads are elsewhere. Emmalisa Sparrow Wood, your editing skills and dependability are in a league of their own. And Kaitlyn Grace, your accuracy and thoughtfulness on the front lines beautifully reminds us that we are all here to serve one another.

Thanks, to each of you, on behalf of myself and the countless people our work will reach.

# About Mike Dooley

*"Mike Dooley is a great messenger of truth; a gift for humanity."*
—don Miguel Ruiz, author of *The Four Agreements*

Mike is a *New York Times* best-selling author, metaphysical teacher, and creator of the popular email received daily by more than one million people, Notes from the Universe, whose acclaimed books—including *Infinite Possibilities: The Art of Living Your Dreams* and *The Top Ten Things Dead People Want to Tell YOU*—have been published worldwide in twenty-seven languages. He was one of the featured teachers in the phenomenon *The Secret* and has presented to live audiences in 156 cities across 42 countries.

You can be informed of Mike's latest works and appearances by subscribing to:

Notes from the Universe[sm]
www.tut.com

*Reflections, insights, and aha! moments*

*Reflections, insights, and aha! moments*

*Reflections, insights, and aha! moments*

*Reflections, insights, and aha! moments*

*Reflections, insights, and aha! moments*

*Reflections, insights, and aha! moments*

*Reflections, insights, and aha! moments*

## TUT's Adventurers Club
## THE UNIVERSE TALKS℠

Launched in 1989 by two brothers and their cool mom, TUT® believes that everyone is special, that every life is meaningful, and that we're all here to learn that dreams really do come true.

We also believe that our *thoughts become things®* and that imagination is the gift that can bring love, health, abundance, and happiness into our lives.

TUT® Enterprises, Inc.
Orlando, Florida
www.tut.com
USA